THE RACKHAM FUNDS
OF THE
UNIVERSITY OF MICHIGAN
1933-1953

HORACE H. RACKHAM

THE RACKHAM FUNDS
OF THE
UNIVERSITY OF MICHIGAN
1933 - 1953

by

SHERIDAN W. BAKER, JR.

ANN ARBOR
UNIVERSITY OF MICHIGAN
1955

Printed and bound by CPI Group (UK) Ltd, Croydon, CR0 4YY

Paperback ISBN: 978-0-472-75014-6

Foreword

Two decades have now passed since the Horace H. Rackham funds were so generously given to the University of Michigan. In keeping with the vision and the wishes of the donors, the funds have been dedicated to significant cultural and humanitarian interests; to the aid of productive scholars and of selected students of high capacity; and to the research programs of the University centering in the Horace H. Rackham School of Graduate Studies.

This book was specially prepared to tell the story of the Rackham funds, to set forth the specific accomplishments and results of the beneficence, and, as it were, to account for twenty years of responsible stewardship in discharging this trust.

The University of Michigan is a stronger institution because of this support, and with these additional resources has been able to make a far richer contribution in the service of mankind than it could otherwise have done.

HARLAN HATCHER

Preface

More than twenty years have passed since the death of Horace H. Rackham in 1933. During his lifetime he made several specific gifts to the University of Michigan amounting to more than a half-million dollars, and after his death the Trustees of the Horace H. Rackham and Mary A. Rackham Fund, which was established by his will, gave the University the splendid buildings and endowments that now bear the Rackham name. From the income of these endowments, the Board of Governors of the Horace H. Rackham School of Graduate Studies has disbursed over four million dollars: for graduate fellowships, for a wide variety of research projects, and for support of a number of agencies within the jurisdiction of the Graduate School.

In 1940 the Trustees published *The Horace H. Rackham and Mary A. Rackham Fund,* describing the many gifts they had made. The University of Michigan was only one of many recipients of these gifts; nevertheless, besides a number of specific grants, large and small, it received from the Trustees four separate endowment funds, as well as the supervision of a fifth, and Mrs. Rackham added a sixth. These funds, together with the two buildings erected in Mr. Rackham's memory, one on the Ann Arbor campus and one in Detroit, are among the greatest educational memorials of our time.

The aim of this report is to clarify the objectives of the endowment funds, which are often indiscriminately referred to, even by University people, as "the Rackham Fund," and to explain what has been accomplished by them and by the agencies they support in carrying out the purposes to which Mr. Rackham dedicated his fortune.

Contents

The Horace H. Rackham and Mary A. Rackham Fund

Horace H. Rackham was a country boy who came to the city, studied law at night, and died a multimillionaire. He was born on June 27, 1858, in Harrison Township, Macomb County, Michigan. His father, Simon Rackham, a retired English sea captain, was a farmer. His mother, Ann Avery Rackham, was a devout Baptist, and he was brought up in the Baptist church, but later in life he and his wife became Christian Scientists. He went to a one-room district school in Harrison Township and to the Union School at Mount Clemens; he graduated from Leslie High School at the age of twenty.

The next year (1879), Horace Rackham went to work for Berry Brothers in Detroit. In 1881, after several jobs, he began reading law in the office of C. K. Latham and was admitted to the bar on June 4, 1884. He married Mary A. Horton of Fenton, Michigan, in 1886. In 1894 he formed, with John W. Anderson, the law firm which was to draw up the articles of incorporation for the Ford Motor Company.

Henry Ford was Horace Rackham's neighbor, but the business of organizing the company (in 1903) was brought to Rackham and Anderson by Alexander G. Malcomson, a coal and wood merchant, who was a client of the law firm and a backer of Ford. Each of the lawyers received a $25 fee.[1] Each borrowed $5,000 for fifty shares of stock—Mr. Anderson, on his insurance policy, Mr. Rackham, on four acres of subdivision partly planted in vegetables, which he grew to supplement his income. Banker C. C. Jenks, when asked for the loan, advised against it on the ground, it is said, that even the bicycle had not displaced the horse.

This was an unusual investment for Horace Rackham, who was opposed to gambling. He himself stated that he handed over his $5,000 with "fear and trembling."[2] He hoped only to get it back. His profits, however, were tremendous. The Ford stock was split twenty for one on November 30, 1908, and when Edsel Ford, as his father's agent, bought up the stock in 1919, the original $28,000 investment in the Ford Motor Company brought $75,000,000.[3] Mr. Rackham sold his 1,000 shares for $12,500,000. By this time his dividends had been about $2,000,000. He died on June 13, 1933—two weeks before his seventy-fifth birthday—owning assets worth $16,611,000, after having given away large sums in his lifetime.

In 1913, fifty-five years old, he had retired to look after his fortune, but he continued his habits of thrift and economy, riding the streetcar to offices in the Dime Bank Building. Nevertheless, he played golf and gave his club a house. He felt the responsibility of his money. His philanthropies were extensive, and when he died he left most of his fortune for general welfare, particularly for

"the sick, aged, young, erring, poor, crippled, helpless, handicapped, unfor‑
tunate, and underprivileged, regardless of race, color, religion or station," for
"the inculcation of thrift, industry, frugality, temperance, self‑reliance, good
citizenship and other cardinal virtues, particularly among the young," for
"wholesome recreation for the people," and for "study, research, and publi‑
cation."

The University's benefits from Horace H. Rackham's fortune began in
1922, although these early, and always anonymous, gifts did not lead directly
to the endowment of the Graduate School after his death. In May, 1922, with
$15,000 from Mr. Rackham, the University bought Greek Biblical manu‑
scripts, largely from the collection—just marketed—of the Baroness Burdett‑
Coutts. In June he began to finance a three‑year anthropological expedition
to the Philippines, at $10,000 a year. Dr. Carl E. Guthe of the University Mu‑
seum was transported from island to island on a ninety‑foot schooner loaned
by Mr. Dean C. Worcester (Michigan '91), who was the first United States
minister to the Philippines, and he collected and brought back Chinese jars
and prehistoric utensils, bones, and gold‑fretted teeth. Mr. Rackham also
gave the University funds to support, with $5,000 each, three Fellows in
Creative Arts: Robert Frost, the American poet (1922–23); Robert Bridges,
then poet laureate of England (1923–24); Jesse Lynch Williams, American
playwright and novelist (1925–26).

Mr. Rackham's friendship with Harry B. Hutchins, President of the Uni‑
versity from 1910 to 1920, and with Francis W. Kelsey, Professor of Latin and
Director of Near East Research, led to gifts totaling $445,000 to the Univer‑
sity's Near Eastern Research Fund, beginning in 1922. With part of this mon‑
ey, the University bought antiquities and enough Greek and Coptic papyri
to make a collection that is equaled or surpassed only by those in London,
in Paris, in Berlin, and in Cairo. When it came on the market in 1924,
the University also bought Sultan Abdul Hamid's collection of fine Arabic
and Persian calligraphy. The largest part of the $445,000, however, went
for excavations in Egypt.

Mr. Rackham had become interested in the possibility of finding Biblical
manuscripts and, in 1924, financed a three‑year expedition by Professor Kelsey
to dig at Kom Aushim, in the Fayoum, Egypt, for the buried city of Karanis.
After Professor Kelsey's death in 1927, Mr. Rackham financed the expedition
for two more three‑year periods. With an additional $50,000 from the Trus‑
tees after Mr. Rackham's death, the University finished work at Karanis in
1934 and began explorations, never completed, at Kom Abou Billou.[4] The
excavations at Karanis drew international attention and produced a wealth
of relics and publications, which, altogether, constitute the most complete
modern account of a Graeco‑Egyptian city. No Biblical manuscripts were
found, however.

In his will Mr. Rackham left the University $100,000 for gifts and loans to students of high character, "especially to those who might not otherwise go to college." This stands today as the Horace H. Rackham Loan Fund, from which, as Mr. Rackham preferred, loans at 3 per cent, rather than gifts, are made. With this bequest the total of Mr. Rackham's personal gifts to the University was brought to $605,000. The first gift made to the University from the Rackham estate came from Mrs. Rackham in July, 1933, when she gave her husband's law library to the Law School.

The Horace H. Rackham and Mary A. Rackham Fund was set up by Mr. Rackham's will for the general benefit of mankind, and there was no designation of the University as an institution to be given preferment. Neither Mr. nor Mrs. Rackham was a Michigan graduate. Yet of the $14,215,413.26[5] in the fund, the University eventually received $9,672,581.85, and Mrs. Rackham added personal gifts amounting to $2,000,000.

Several factors account for the University's large share in the Rackham estate. The Trustees[6] recognized in the University an institution already engaged in the education and the research they were commissioned to support. Moreover, when the newspapers announced the terms of the bequest, Alexander G. Ruthven, President of the University (1929–51), realizing that many of the University faculty would apply for research grants, wrote Judge Arthur J. Lacy, one of the Trustees (June 27, 1933), asking that all requests from the University staff be passed over the President's desk, and adding: "Sometime . . . I will take occasion to discuss with you what, in my opinion, is one of the most important problems in the State." President Ruthven had in mind a large, single endowment to the University for research in all departments. In September, President Ruthven received a letter from Mr. Bryson D. Horton, executor of the will and brother of Mrs. Rackham, saying: "As one of the trustees of the Horace H. and Mary A. Rackham Fund and as an alumnus of the University of Michigan, I personally, am very desirous that a substantial amount be appropriated from this fund for research in various fields." Soon the Trustees approached President Ruthven for advice, and they made a tour of the large endowed Foundations at his suggestion.

After several conferences, President Ruthven made definite proposals (October 2, 1933). He suggested "something comparable to a good-sized house in Ann Arbor in which offices of the administrators and council rooms could be provided, with the tremendous facilities of the University at hand . . . ." He further suggested a "combined board of 'foundation' people and University people to pass on research to be done in various fields." He recommended a "wide spread of research and . . . particular attention to the preparation of the men and women who are coming on to run the world for better or worse rather than . . . supporting projects which are merely palliative in their effect."

On January 1, 1934, the Horace H. Rackham and Mary A. Rackham Fund became operative, and in the following June executive offices were opened in Ann Arbor under the directorship of Dr. Mark S. Knapp. During 1934, 1935, and the early part of 1936, the Trustees made numerous grants, a generous share of them to the University. In 1934 they gave the Graduate School $13,500 for graduate research fellowships. In 1934 and 1935 they made a number of grants for faculty research projects, which, with one made early in 1936, amounted to $219,881.85; these are described in detail later. They also gave sums totaling $55,700 to inaugurate or assist other important activities of the University.[7]

In 1936 the interest of the Trustees turned more particularly to buildings and endowments that would promote the work of the Graduate School and, at the same time, serve as a memorial to Mr. Rackham.

The Horace H. Rackham School of Graduate Studies

President Ruthven and the Trustees had been holding conferences about a major endowment, and on March 26, 1935, the President wrote to Mr. Horton:

> Since our conversation last week, I have given considerable thought to the matter we discussed. I want to propose a plan to you which I believe will challenge your interest. What I have to offer to you and the other Trustees of the Rackham Fund is no less than the very heart of the University.
>
> The research center of the institution is, of course, the Graduate School. At the present time, and from now on, the researches of members of the staff and graduate students and the encouragement of graduate studies will center in this school. With some assistance the Graduate School could become an outstanding section of the University which would command the admiration of the entire world. The progress made up to the present time has been remarkable but there are needed now certain facilities which are not available. For example, we need fellowships, money for research, and a place for the students and faculty to come together.
>
> Concretely, my proposal would be that the Rackham Fund set aside $5,000,000 to be used as follows: $1,000,000 or $1,250,000 for the erection and equipment of a building . . ., this building to be maintained by the University; the balance of the appropriation to be in the form of an endowment for fellowships and the expenses of research. Further, I would suggest that the Graduate School be known as the Rackham School of Graduate Studies of the University of Michigan.

On September 7, 1935, the Regents of the University agreed with the Rackham Trustees to name the Graduate School and the building the "Horace H. Rackham School of Graduate Studies" and to accept $4,000,000 as an endowment for research and $1,000,000 for the building. At the time this agreement was signed, President Ruthven, with the Trustees' approval, had already entered into negotiations for the purchase of the land for the new Graduate School Building. Options had been taken on the block (mostly old houses turned into apartments) now under the eastern half of the Rackham building, and the purchase was completed before the end of that month. Mrs. Rackham, however, strongly favored more extensive grounds, believing that the single block of land would not provide an appropriate setting for the memorial building she envisaged, and on November 1, 1935, the Trustees added $1,500,000 to buy the block to the west, to close Ingalls street, to expand grounds and building, and to center the building directly opposite the flagpole and Library. The total amount allotted for the grounds, building, and furnishings was, then, $2,500,000. The contractors agreed to construct the building for $1,560,000, but they were able to do it for $13,000 less than that figure.

The cornerstone was laid October 30, 1936. Smith, Hinchman, and Grylls of Detroit, represented by William E. Kapp, designed the building; the W. E.

5

Wood Company of Detroit built it; William J. Pitkin, Jr., and Seward II. Mott did the landscaping; Joseph Parducci did the exterior sculpture. Carleton W. Angell, Artist, University Museums, modeled the bronze portrait plaque of Mr. Rackham that was placed in the circular foyer on the second floor, and Professor John G. Winter, Director of the Museum of Classical Archaeology and a friend of Mr. Rackham, wrote the memorial inscription that is set in bronze letters beneath it:

HORACE H. RACKHAM
1858–1933

POVERTY DID NOT EMBITTER HIM NOR WEALTH AFFECT THE SIMPLICITY OF HIS LIFE AND THE EVEN TENOR OF HIS WAY. HIS MIND MOVED ALWAYS ON A HIGH PLANE, SERENE AND NOBLE, AND HIS VISION EXTENDED TO THE PROBLEMS OF HUMAN SUFFERING AND HAPPINESS EVERYWHERE. . . . . HIS BROAD HUMANITARIANISM AND HIS PERVADING WISDOM REMAIN A LIVING FORCE, HIS MEMORY A REFRESHING INSPIRATION. . . . .

The building was dedicated on June 17, 1938. It stands not only as a monument to Mr. Rackham, but as a symbol of the magnitude of the Rackham endowment, among the largest single grants ever made to a university in the United States. Of Indiana limestone, with copper roof, granite base course, and bronze door and window framing, it holds libraries, offices, research rooms, lounges, reception rooms, small serving rooms, a small auditorium, and a large lecture hall. It is rich and spacious, with furniture following the designs of Chippendale and Duncan Phyfe and upholstered in leather and tapestries. The décor mingles Grecian and Pompeian influences; the supposition that Mr. Rackham's Egyptian interests were responsible for the decorations in the Lecture Hall is unfounded.

The Lecture Hall, the architectural heart of the building, is acoustically superb, and it has become the center for almost daily lectures, conferences, conventions, and concerts. Here, each year, numerous conferences of nationwide importance are held. The arrangement of the 1,200 comfortable seats in semicircular rows, with ample leg room between, makes it unusually attractive for such gatherings, facilitating, as it does, discussion from the floor.

Over thirty learned societies and departments of the University use the building regularly for meetings and conferences, often held in the Amphitheater on the third floor, a small auditorium reflecting the beauty and the practical features of the large Lecture Hall. The Graduate Student Council and other groups use the rooms for meetings and for social functions for graduate students. In the Reading Room on the second floor, graduate students find a quiet place for study, or they may stop in the lounges for record concerts, conversation, and relaxation. Each year thousands of townspeople, faculty members, and students attend free concerts of the University's Stanley Quartet and other chamber-music groups from the School of Music, and almost all recitals of vocalists and instrumentalists for the Master's Degree in the School of Music are presented in one or another of the Rackham rooms or reception halls. University and local artists, as well as the art classes of the Ann Arbor public schools, hold several exhibits annually in galleries on the mezzanine floor. In the Assembly Hall on the third floor, various departments of the University hold their receptions and teas. The Board Room, where the Board of Governors and the Executive Board hold their meetings, and the administrative offices of the Graduate School are situated in the building.

The agreement that had resulted in the building and endowment had defined the purposes for which they could be used. It had provided also for a Board of Governors of the Graduate School as part of the administrative organization. This Board was to be made up of the President of the University, Chairman, the Dean of the Graduate School (both ex officio), and three appointees to be designated by the Trustees and to serve for life, subject to disability, resignation, or failure to act. The Board of Governors was formally established by the Regents at its meeting in February, 1936, the three appointees being Bryson D. Horton, Detroit, Clarence E. Wilcox, Detroit, and Frederick G. Rolland, Detroit. Its function was to control and direct "the use, expenditure, allocation, and disposition of the Endowment Fund," within the terms of the will of Horace H. Rackham.

At about the time the Trustees had begun to give serious consideration to extensive support for the work of the Graduate School, Dean G. Carl Huber died (December, 1934), and in January, 1935, Clarence S. Yoakum, then Vice-President of the University and Director of Educational Investigations, became Vice-President of the University in Charge of Educational Investigations and Dean of the Graduate School. Later in January, the Regents appointed Peter Okkelberg, then Professor of Zoology and Secretary of the Graduate School, to be Assistant Dean. These two men brought to the administration of the Graduate School close association with the central administration of the University, on the one hand, and familiarity with the operations of the Graduate School, on the other—an effective combination for meeting the changes which the new building and the increase in the money to be disbursed were likely to bring about.

The Executive Board of the Graduate School, composed of ten members of the Graduate School faculty, the Assistant Dean, and the Dean, as Chairman, had been set up to pass upon and make recommendations to the Board of Regents on all matters concerned with the educational policies of the Graduate School, including requirements for admission, requirements for graduation, curriculums, and recommendations for the several graduate degrees. It also made recommendations for fellowship awards, and on the basis of the reports of the Divisional Committees on Research, made recommendations for research grants from the Faculty Research Fund. This Board was continued without change in function, but in the case of the fellowship and research grants made from the Horace H. Rackham Fund (the original $4,000,000 endowment) the recommendations were transmitted to the Board of Governors and, upon their approval, were transmitted by the Dean to the Regents.

On April 27, 1936, the Board of Governors met for the first time. At President Ruthven's invitation the meeting was held in the century-old President's home on the campus of the University of Michigan, with the President, as had been provided, as Chairman, and Dean Yoakum as Secretary. After attending to routine business matters, the Board discussed methods of evaluating scholarly projects forwarded for its approval by the Executive Board. The Chairman reported receipt of $100,000 from the Horace H. Rackham and Mary A. Rackham Fund for research grants, fellowships, and necessary expenses, since the income from the endowment fund was not yet available, and the first grants for fellowships and for faculty research projects under the new organization were then made by the Board and forwarded to the Regents for final approval. Later, as other Rackham endowment funds were given to the University by the Trustees, certain responsibilities for them were delegated to the Board of Governors, for the Trustees were foreseeing the time when all the money in the Horace H. Rackham and Mary A. Rackham Fund would be disposed of and they would be ready to dissolve—as they did on July 10, 1950.

The organization and administration of the Horace H. Rackham School of Graduate Studies have remained essentially unchanged, although there has been an almost complete change in personnel. Upon the death of Dean Yoakum, in November, 1945, Assistant Dean Okkelberg agreed to act as Dean until the appointment of a successor. In the fall of 1946, Ralph A. Sawyer, Professor of Physics, who had been on leave as a Navy commander in charge of the Experimental Laboratories at the Naval Proving Ground and, in the spring and summer of 1946, had been civilian Technical Director for the atomic bomb tests at Bikini, returned to the University as Dean of the Graduate School, and Professor Okkelberg became Associate Dean. When Clifford Woody, Professor of Education, who had served as Graduate Adviser to the Michigan Colleges of Education for ten years, died in December, 1948, Harlan C. Koch, Professor of Education, was appointed Assistant Dean (January, 1949), to take over this work and also to be in charge of the off-campus units of the Graduate School. When, in February, 1950, Associate Dean Okkelberg retired, becoming Associate Dean Emeritus, Robert S. Ford, Professor of

Economics, was also appointed Assistant Dean (May, 1950), to be in charge of admissions and student relations.

In August, 1951, President Ruthven retired, becoming President Emeritus, and in September, Harlan Hatcher, then Vice-President of the Ohio State University, became President and, ex officio, the Chairman of the Board of Governors. Mr. Horton's death, in 1945, and Mr. Rolland's death, in 1946, created vacancies which were filled by Charles L. Bussey, of Detroit, and J. Burns Fuller, of Fenton. While President Emeritus Ruthven and Associate Dean Emeritus Okkelberg are still keenly interested in the activities and progress of the Graduate School, Mr. Clarence E. Wilcox, one of the original Trustees of the Horace H. Rackham and Mary A. Rackham Fund and a member of the Board of Governors since its establishment, is the only one now connected with its work who had a part in the early negotiations that brought what have proved to be ever-increasing benefits to the Graduate School and to the University.

In the twenty years since the first gifts from the Horace H. Rackham and Mary A. Rackham Fund were made to the Graduate School, its growth and development have done much to fulfill the hopes that President Ruthven and the Trustees had for it. The intervening years have encompassed the period of World War II, when a large part of the potential graduate student body was diverted to war activities, and the years following the war when there was a great surge of students back to their interrupted education. This wave of students has subsided, and the new wave, building up from the high birth rate of the forties, has not yet reached the graduate schools. In this respect, conditions now are rather like those of the middle thirties; but even so, the graduate student body is more than three times as large as it was then.

In the first semester of 1934–35, 1,226 students were enrolled in the Graduate School, about 200 of whom were studying in the Center for Graduate Studies in Detroit; in that year, 90 doctor's degrees and 571 master's degrees were conferred. The first semester of 1953–54 saw 4,042 students in the Graduate School, about 1,300 of whom were enrolled in the five Centers for Graduate Study and the co-operative programs conducted at the Northern and Central Michigan Colleges of Education. During the school year of 1952–53, 265 doctor's degrees and 1,423 master's degrees were conferred. The Horace H. Rackham School of Graduate Studies was third among the graduate schools of the nation in the number of master's degrees conferred, and seventh in the number of doctor's degrees.

This increase in the number of students and in the number of degrees conferred has been paralleled by the increase in the number of graduate faculty members and in the extent and variety of their research activities. Much of this research has been stimulated and assisted by the Rackham Funds; they have been a strong influence for a high level of scholarly activity throughout the University.

The Institute for Human Adjustment

As early as 1935, the Trustees had indicated their interest in supporting some project, in conjunction with the University, for the care of the aged. Their original idea was for a convalescent home. Dr. Knapp, himself, favored a maternity hospital because, as he stated in a letter to President Ruthven, August 26, 1935, he was inclined "to believe it will better fit in with Mrs. Rackham's religious belief . . . ." President Ruthven replied (August 28, 1935): "Why not a 'Mary A. Rackham Home' devoted to rehabilitation in all phases: to teach the deaf to read lips, to teach the aged man vocations and avocations, to care for indigent and expectant mothers, to rehabilitate the injured, etc." In a letter dated December 9, 1935, President Ruthven mentions "my dream for an institute for human adjustment."

On June 3, 1936, President Ruthven proposed a $1,000,000 endowment to start the rehabilitation center. On June 11, the Regents accepted a personal gift of $1,000,000 from Mrs. Rackham for the rehabilitation of those—the aged, the sick, the unemployed—who are not self-sufficient members of society. From the Horace H. Rackham and Mary A. Rackham Fund, the Trustees made available to the University up to $75,000 (accepted by the Regents on June 19) for a building and equipment. The Board of Governors of the Graduate School on June 20, 1936, accepted the responsibility for a list of fifty-seven pensioners (relatives and friends of the Rackhams) that had been carried by the Trustees, their pensions, amounting in all to about $18,000 a year, to be paid from the income of the new $1,000,000 Mary A. Rackham Fund. With this exception, however, the Board resolved to use the income from Mrs. Rackham's gift entirely for a "social service center." The initial $4,000,000 from the Horace H. Rackham and Mary A. Rackham Fund, given as an endowment for the Horace H. Rackham School of Graduate Studies, then became the Horace H. Rackham Fund.

By fall, 1936, the new project was no longer "the social service center" but, in President Ruthven's earlier phrase, "The Institute for Human Adjustment."[8] The University already had a Speech Clinic that was pursuing some of the problems suggested in President Ruthven's earliest plans. During the summer the Psi Omega fraternity house had been purchased for $15,000 with part of the $75,000 building grant. A search of title showed that the fraternity had never owned a strip between the house and the street (the street had not been laid out exactly as planned) and that the University owned an island with no bridge; $300 more bought the frontage. In the winter of 1936 renovation began; by June, 1937, the furnishings and equipment had been installed and the Speech Clinic moved in (where it remains today) as the first unit of the Institute for Human Adjustment. In April, 1937, because the income from Mrs. Rackham's $1,000,000 gift was not yet available to the University, the Trustees had given $100,000 from the Horace H. Rackham and Mary A. Rackham Fund for the early expenses of the Institute. Later, in 1940, they gave an additional $100,000, also for expenses. In 1939, they earmarked for the Institute for Human Adjustment the income from an addition to the Horace H. Rackham Fund of $400,000 which they had set aside to cover any final claims against the Rackham estate, a precaution that had turned out to be unnecessary. This came to the University on December 31, 1941.

In February, 1938, the Board of Governors appointed Mr. Clark Tibbitts Director of the Institute. He had earlier been an Instructor in the Department of Sociology and had become an expert on community leadership. He, Dean Yoakum, and Mrs. Mary H. Church, who had succeeded Dr. Knapp as Director of the Horace H. Rackham and Mary A. Rackham Fund, became the Executive Committee for the expanded Institute.[9]

Today, the Executive Committee is made up of six members of the faculty appointed by the Executive Board of the Graduate School, with Dean Sawyer as Chairman. The committee meets once a month to consider and pass upon all matters pertaining to the activities of the Institute. Dean Sawyer also acts as Director of the Institute, and Mr. Woodrow Hunter, Research Associate in Gerontology, serves, part-time, as Administrative Assistant to the Director.

The Speech Clinic

The Speech Clinic, one of the first in the field, continues to be one of the best in the United States. It receives its support from the income of the Mary A. Rackham Fund, from University funds through the Department of Speech for teaching services, and from the fees of its clients. Professor Harlan H. Bloomer, who succeeded Professor J. H. Muyskens in the fall of 1939, directs a clinical and teaching staff of about twelve, including, besides speech correctionists, a physician, a social caseworker, and a clinical psychologist. The Clinic aims to bring as many skills as possible to bear upon the speech problems of the patient, avoiding the inefficiency of sending him here and there for professional advice on the separate aspects of his whole problem.

The Clinic provides training for graduate students as experts in aiding those with defective hearing and as speech correctionists, and it provides case material for the research and training of speech scientists. There are a number of candidates for master's and doctor's degrees working in the Clinic each year. Each year, also, some six hundred adults and children from all parts of the United States receive aid in their hearing difficulties or in one or another of the eight speech disorders treated: (1) articulatory disorders (defects in the pronunciation of vowels and consonants), (2) stuttering, (3) voice disorders having to do with pitch, intensity, and quality, including those caused by the surgical removal of the larynx, the patient learning to speak by a remarkable process of eructation shaped into words by mouth and tongue; (4) delayed speech in children, (5) aphasia (loss of speech due to brain injury), (6) speech difficulties caused by or related to cleft palate, or (7) cerebral palsy, or (8) hearing loss. The Clinic's distinctive development is its program in group therapy, especially for aphasics, which is far ahead of anything in the country. Groups of ten or twelve—one group of aphasics grew to twenty-eight, a number too large for effective treatment—attend classes for eight weeks, five hours a day, five days a week. Applications indicate that the program has gained a national reputation.

Shady Trails, the University of Michigan Speech Improvement Camp (near Northport), also has a connection with Rackham gifts to the University. Mr. John M. Clancy founded the camp with four boys in 1932; in September, 1937, he joined the Speech Clinic on a part-time basis and now serves as Assistant to the Director. Between 1934 and 1940 the Rackham Trustees gave the camp a total of $15,000 in yearly grants. On March 1, 1949, the University bought Shady Trails with a grant from the Kresge Foundation. The camp is not directly connected with the Speech Clinic nor with the Institute for Human Adjustment. It is carried on the University's Summer Session budget, and it has never been assisted by the University's Rackham funds. Nevertheless, the gift of $15,000 by the Trustees of the Rackham estate helped it in its early years. Mr. Clancy continues to direct it, and each summer several students receive internships in speech correction, their tuition, room, and board being paid by the Camp. Similar camps have appeared and disappeared, but Shady Trails continues to be one of the best. Each summer, some ninety-six boys, representing about twenty-five states, go through nine weeks of training in enunciation, social adjustment, and body building, with outstandingly favorable results.

The Bureau of Psychological Services

The history of the Bureau of Psychological Services may be traced back to a time considerably earlier than the endowment of the Institute for Human Adjustment by Mrs. Rackham. In fact, there were two quite independent, precursory activities in this field: one, a program of psychological testing of University students started in the fall of 1927 by Professor Clarence S. Yoakum and running for some years parallel to the Bureau before joining it; the other, the Michigan Child Guidance Institute.

In 1933 (coincidentally, the year of Mr. Rackham's death) President Ruthven, Professor Lowell J. Carr of the Department of Sociology, and other citizens of Ann Arbor formed a committee to look into the alleviation of child delinquency. Several on this committee, known as the President's Treatment-Planning Committee, were actively interested in the Fresh Air Camp for underprivileged and delinquent boys, which the University eventually acquired in 1944. During the academic year 1933–34, Professor Carr, on sabbatical leave, made a survey of conditions aggravating delinquency in towns and cities throughout the state, and he also proposed a study of the effectiveness of the Fresh Air Camp. His proposal resulted in a gift to the University from the Rackham Trustees—among their first gifts—of $5,000 (May 18, 1934) for research into juvenile delinquency. From this Rackham grant developed the University's Michigan Juvenile Delinquency Information Service, directed by Professor Carr, which conducted research and published a monthly *Delinquency News Letter* that was sent to more than eight thousand agencies and persons in all parts of Michigan. To support this service, the Rackham Trustees added $7,000 on May 31, 1935, and the *Delinquency News Letter* continued a lively existence from its beginning in August, 1936, until June, 1940.

The Michigan Juvenile Delinquency Information Service, itself, was soon to be supplanted by the Michigan Child Guidance Institute, sponsored by State Senator Herbert P. Orr and Professor John P. Dawson of the University's Law School. Professor Carr and many others assisted in framing the plan, and Senator Orr's bill to create the Michigan Child Guidance Institute became Act No. 285, Public Acts of 1937. On October 29, 1937, the Regents accepted the responsibility of acting as the Board of Trustees for the Institute, naming Professor Carr as Director. Professor Carr opened offices in Ann Arbor, and a Field Study Unit, consisting of a psychologist and two social caseworkers, began research and advisory work, principally in Oakland, Monroe, and Clinton counties. The state provided about $38,000 a year.

The Michigan Child Guidance Institute, however, remained active for only a few years. Other agencies were undertaking similar functions; for example, Professor Carr's Ann Arbor Boy's Guidance Project, started in 1935 with an $18,000 gift to the University from the Rackham Trustees to support the study of problem children in the Ann Arbor schools and at the Fresh Air Camp,[10] was taken over by the community as the Ann Arbor Children's Service Bureau in 1938. Work with children by the Neuropsychiatric Institute of the University Hospital had grown considerably. Moreover, the outbreak of the war in 1941 had dimmed the problems of juvenile delinquency for a great many citizens and for many members of the state legislature. Consequently, Professor Carr recommended to the Governor that the Michigan Child Guidance Institute be discontinued, its functions being adequately handled by the state departments of Welfare and of Correction, by private agencies, and, at the University, by the Neuropsychiatric Institute and the Psychological Clinic.

The Michigan Child Guidance Institute went out of existence on June 30, 1943.

Although the Michigan Child Guidance Institute had no direct connection with the establishment of either the Bureau of Psychological Services or the Institute for Human Adjustment, work with the delinquency program helped direct the thinking of the Rackham Trustees and of President Ruthven toward problems of adjustment and toward a psychological clinic. Dean Yoakum provided the plans for such a clinic. As has been mentioned, Dean Yoakum, a psychologist noted for his development and administration of psychological testing for the United States Army during World War I, had been conducting a program of testing and evaluating University students, and Professor Charles H. Griffitts had approached him about the possibility of a clinical program of psychological research. At Dean Yoakum's instance, President Ruthven proposed such a clinic to the Rackham Trustees. The Speech Clinic was already almost filling the Psi Omega house, originally bought for the whole Institute, and since it had cost only about a third of the money made available for the purchase, President Ruthven suggested that the Trustees authorize buying another house, just down the street, for the proposed Psychological Clinic and the program of testing children for the Michigan Child Guidance Institute, already being conducted by University psychologists. Concerning this program, President Ruthven wrote the Trustees (November 9, 1937): "While supported by the State, it is really a part of the program of the Institute for Human Adjustment." In January, 1938, the Trustees assigned $25,000 from the original $75,000 building grant for the house at 1027 East Huron (today the Psychological Clinic, Bureau of Psychological Services, Institute for Human Adjustment), and in February the Clinic was established. It took over the testing program for the Michigan Child Guidance Institute, for which it received $1,000 a year, and when the Institute went out of existence in 1943, the valuable store of case records was turned over to the Clinic.[11]

The Psychological Clinic has kept its house and has retained its identity, but it eventually evolved into the Bureau of Psychological Services, which includes the Clinic within its broader organization. This evolution progressed in four stages. First came the development of the Clinic under the direction of Professor Charles H. Griffitts, who was then a member of the Executive Committee of the Michigan Child Guidance Institute. Professor Griffitts worked out a comprehensive program of clinical study and counseling, covering thousands of school children in Ann Arbor, Port Huron, Ypsilanti, and other Michigan towns. In the fall of 1939, the Graduate School offered, for the first time, a degree in clinical psychology, the degree of Master of Clinical Psychology based upon a two-year course of study including a one-semester internship in the field. A number of graduate students were housed as interns in the Juvenile Home at Pontiac and elsewhere and were visited for weekly conferences by a field team from the Clinic. One of the significant products of the Clinic's research was Dr. Wilma T. Donahue's *The Measurement of Student Adjustment and Achievement.*[12]

The war and Professor Griffitts' resignation as Director, on October 16, 1944, introduced the second phase of the Clinic's development, one of retrenchment and of dwindling staff and students. Work continued under Dr. Donahue as ranking staff member, without title. As the war ended and students began to flow back to the University, Dr. Donahue began plans for an expanded psychological service.

On September 28, 1945, when the Clinic took over the student-testing program, the third stage in its evolution began. It was then renamed the Bureau of Psychological Services to indicate its widened scope. The Regents appointed Dr. Donahue Director of the new Bureau on July 1, 1946.[13] Shortly thereafter, she separated the work which the Clinic had been doing into four divisions: the Psychological Clinic, a Testing Division, a Research Division, and a Counseling Division. On June 30, 1949, Dr. Donahue resigned to head the program in gerontology that was being started by the Institute for Human Adjustment, and for a year the Bureau operated under the guidance of Professor Clyde H. Coombs, Chief of the Research Division, as ranking member of the staff. Professor E. Lowell Kelly became Director on August 19, 1950, and the fourth stage of development began.

Today Professor Kelly administers the Bureau's four divisions from his offices in Haven Hall: (1) the Student Counseling Division, (2) the Evaluation and Examining Division, (3) the Division of Reading Improvement Services, (4) the Psychological Clinic. In all divisions the Bureau continues its threefold program: research, training graduate students, and helping people in the early identification and alleviation of their special problems. The Bureau receives $22,000 annually from the income of the Mary A. Rackham Fund, and it receives money from the University, also, for its services to students; the Counseling Division and the Psychological Clinic collect some fees.

The Student Counseling Division, of which Associate Professor Edward S. Bordin is Chief, concentrates on aiding students and prospective students, through interviews, to make their own decisions on educational and vocational problems; in addition, it extends services to people outside the University who are referred by the Veterans Administration and the State Vocational Rehabilitation Service, and to a few private citizens. For these services fees are charged.

The Evaluation and Examining Division, of which Assistant Professor Edward J. Furst is Chief, conducts standard aptitude tests for all incoming freshmen, thus aiding academic counselors throughout the University, and it assists faculty members in constructing and evaluating examinations and in grading objective examinations. It has recently investigated the backgrounds of the ablest students, their distribution among University departments, and the relative standing of transfer students. This Division also serves the public schools of Michigan with testing and consultation.

During its first year of operation, the Division of Reading Improvement Services, organized in September, 1952, helped 447 students and faculty members, trained reading supervisors, and conducted statistical analyses of techniques and results. On the basis of this study, Dr. Donald E. P. Smith, Chief of the Division, found that no correlation appears between intelligence and the degree of improvement in reading skill; that the students who work most conscientiously are those who improve least—although they do improve; and that the key to this puzzle is probably anxiety, since those students most concerned over poor reading and poor grades have the greatest difficulty in improving their reading skill.

The Psychological Clinic, with Professor Frederick Wyatt as Chief, carries on a program of research and graduate training in clinical psychology and service to the public at large, for which, as in the case of the counseling service, fees are charged. It has recently initiated a program to acquaint local religious and welfare leaders with its work. Its calendar of appointments is crowded.

Since its beginnings in 1937 and 1938, the Bureau of Psychological Services, with its four subdivisions, has grown notably in size and in effectiveness. It is providing needed services to the University and the community, as well as opportunities for research and training in fields of great importance in our modern world.

The Social Science Research Project

One of the major operations of the Michigan Juvenile Delinquency Information Service, established, as noted earlier, by gifts from the Rackham Trustees, was a research project conducted in Flint, Michigan, by Mrs. Minna Faust, which resulted in her 224-page report, "Juvenile Delinquency in Flint in the Light of Social, Economic, and Cultural Factors 1925–1934." Perhaps partly for this reason, when the Rackham Trustees decided to continue their support for the University's research into juvenile delinquency, they chose Flint as their testing ground; they may also have been influenced by the fact that four of the Trustees, Mrs. Rackham, Mrs. Bussey, Mr. Horton, and Mr. Rolland, had grown up in the neighborhood of Flint, where, to their concern, rapid industrialization had noticeably altered the environment and the pattern of childhood and youth.

On May 1, 1938, the Trustees gave the University $500,000 for a Sociological Research Fund, under the jurisdiction of the Graduate School, to finance the study of vocational guidance, juvenile delinquency, and other sociological and community problems. They added $5,000 in July, for expenses. The study was to be conducted "primarily in Flint" for the first five years; then the Board of Governors would be free to change to other communities.

On October 17, 1938, the Sociological Research Unit, as it was called, was placed by the Board of Governors within the Institute for Human Adjustment, with support still to be provided by the Rackham Sociological Research Fund. The Institute worked out with the Flint schools a program of vocational guidance, established graduate fellowships for research into community problems, started files of statistics and tests, and trained social workers. Although significant aid to the community was rendered and a number of University graduate students were trained, interest in the Flint project declined. The early annual budgets of about $17,000 had been reduced to a little more than $6,000 by May, 1943; from time to time, however, a number of people on University salaries continued to do research in Flint. The Rackham Trustees and the Board of Governors of the Graduate School had hoped that the Flint project would demonstrate its value sufficiently for Flint to adopt it as its own, but although the community appreciated the service, it was not until May, 1946, that any money came to the project from Flint. At that time, the C. S. Mott Foundation and the Industrial Mutual Association of Flint provided $2,500 each, and the Flint Community Trust Fund, $5,000.

At the same time, the Flint project was reorganized and became integrated with the University's Metropolitan Community Seminar, which had been initiated in 1931 by Professor R. D. McKenzie, of the Department of Sociology, and continued under the direction of a committee, of which Professor Amos H. Hawley, also of the Department of Sociology, was chairman. The Seminar brought together men from the departments of City Planning, Economics, Geography, Political Science, Public Administration, and Sociology to teach and to direct graduate research into all urban problems. Under the new arrangement, it continued to conduct its seminar on the Ann Arbor campus but used the already-established field office in Flint as its research center. The former Sociological Research Unit was renamed the Social Science Research Project, with Professor Hawley as Director. Each year, the Seminar enrolls about six graduate fellows from the different departments to study a variety of problems of the Flint Community and its growing suburbs. Mr. Victor Roterus became the Resident Director in Flint on October 15, 1946, and at the end of the year, the Director of the Project reported that Mr. Roterus "did much to acquaint the local people with the purposes of the project and to guide fellowship students." At the request of the Director, the Executive Board of the Graduate School established an advisory board of nine interested Flint citizens. On February 28, 1948, Mr. Roterus left the Project to become an Analyst on the staff of the Department of Commerce in Washington.

On October 1, 1948, his successor, Dr. J. Douglas Carroll, Jr., began four years of highly productive directorship at Flint, showing marked ability to work effectively both in the community and at the University. One of his main projects was an analysis of automobile traffic within the city.[14] In March, 1953, Dr. Carroll resigned to supervise a traffic analysis for the city of Detroit, and Mr. Basil Zimmer was appointed Resident Director, beginning with the first semester of 1953.

As with all divisions of the Institute for Human Adjustment, the Flint Project is a field laboratory for graduate study which functions through service to the public outside the University. An example of the extensive research emanating from the Project is to be found in Dr. Donald J. Bogue's monograph, *The Structure of the Metropolitan Community* (Ann Arbor, 1948), an analysis of various facets of metropolitan life and of their radiation outward to communities beyond, a pattern repeated throughout the United States.

The Social Science Research Project was a pioneer in the co-operation of universities with communities for the purpose of dealing with social problems, and other universities have used it as a model. It has aided the local schools in vocational counseling, studied population shifts between city and country, and evaluated transportation and shopping centers. In conjunction with the Urban League of Flint, it has measured the power of local leadership in given neighborhoods, and, with the Clara Elizabeth Fund, has worked to improve maternal health. Here the Project has developed techniques and knowledge that are already being applied in other Michigan communities.

The University of Michigan Fresh Air Camp

In the summer of 1921, Mr. Lewis C. Reimann, a former Michigan student, the Presbyterian worker among students at the University, and a staff member of the Student Christian Association, founded a camp for underprivileged boys on Patterson Lake in the Pinckney State Recreation Area, twenty-four miles northwest of Ann Arbor. Volunteer student leaders operated the camp. The grant to the University from the Rackham estate for juvenile-delinquency research at the camp ($18,000, May, 1935) has already been noted. At the same time, the Trustees began yearly gifts to the camp itself, amounting to $14,500 by 1940. From 1940 to 1946, the camp was run with severely limited funds. University students continued to assist as volunteers, and they raised money each year by the street-corner sale of lapel tags on a regular tag day, which has now become an established institution. Dr. Ferdinand N. Menefee, Professor of Engineering Mechanics, directed the camp through most of its formative years.

With the Summer Session of 1939, the University began to offer academic credit to the camp counselors. This date may be taken as the beginning of a gradual change in the camp's function: whereas formerly its sole purpose was to provide a supervised vacation for underprivileged boys, today it is a sociological laboratory, serving only maladjusted and aberrant boys selected by social agencies throughout the state.

On June 12, 1944, the Regents accepted from the Virginia R. Ives Association a gift of the camp at Patterson Lake "originally acquired at the cost of $12,000 on which there have been accumulating buildings and equipment to an amount conservatively estimated at $50,000." The Regents accepted the gift of land and buildings with the understanding that University expenditures at the camp would not exceed the $2,500 currently budgeted "in providing instruction at the camp for students in social service."

On January 2, 1946, the University of Michigan Fresh Air Camp was placed in the Institute for Human Adjustment, and so once more began to receive Rackham money—at first from the Mary A. Rackham Fund set up from Mrs. Rackham's million-dollar gift for social rehabilitation, the basic endowment of the Institute, but in a few months, from the Rackham Sociological Research Fund, instead. Mr. William C. Morse (now Associate Professor) became director in February, 1946. University students sit on the Camp advisory committee, raise considerable money, and in the off-season have the use of the facilities for organized groups, for which fees are charged to cover the extra expense. Fees for the Fresh Air campers come from the social agencies sending them, and about cover the cost of their food; the University Summer Session and the Rackham Sociological Research Fund provide academic, administrative, and maintenance costs. Nevertheless, contributions from many charitable people, together with the student campaigns, take care of about one-third of the total expenditures.

The Camp reaches an almost perfect balance between the social rehabilitation of the boys and the training of advanced students in the University's departments of Education, Sociology, Social Work, and Psychology. Between thirty-five and forty-five students from these departments, and some from other universities, work as counselors each summer, beginning with a week's indoctrination before the two four-week sessions. The Department of Psychology urges all those considering graduate work in clinical psychology to undertake a summer of camp experience, and two research assistantships at the Camp are awarded each summer to advanced graduate students in clinical psychology. Students in the School of Social Work do three or four field-work assignments with social agencies, of which the Fresh Air Camp may be one. The other participating departments also encourage this field training. The graduate students function principally as cabin counselors, each with eight boys, but they also function as specialized counselors in art, nature study, sports, dramatics, music, and handicraft, as casework counselors dealing with the knotty problems of social adjustment, as research assistants, as interns in clinical psychology, and as interns in the School of Education's remedial tutoring program.

A permanent staff, including the director, case workers, and experts in all phases of summer camping, supervises the Camp program. Activities are in all ways like those of any summer camp, and about two hundred and forty maladjusted boys between the ages of seven and fourteen are sent from all parts of Michigan by their supervising social agencies for the fun of a summer outing, covering one or the other of two four-week periods. As in all such group activities, a very few are unhappy and leave before the end of the four weeks, but many would like to stay longer and a few are kept for eight weeks if the experience is proving especially helpful.

The boys fall generally into two categories: those with neuroses that cause them to withdraw from a society which seems hostile, and those who make opportunities to fight the restrictions of society. The counselors take the place of the parents, the child's representatives of the adult world, and the group provides him a social unit within which to find himself. Case workers sustain whatever person-to-person therapy is needed in addition to the group therapy, which is the counselors' province.

The boy's social agency sends to the Camp his case history, and the nightly reports on each boy by the counselors are incorporated in reports sent back to the agency at the end of the camping period. Each week the counselors and staff hold a diagnostic roundtable to study selected cases, with the assistance of Dr. Ralph Rabinovitch, Associate Professor of Psychiatry, in charge of the Children's Service at the Neuropsychiatric Institute of the University Hospital. He synthesizes the findings of counselors and case workers, interviews the child under discussion, and provides diagnosis and recommendations for treatment and procedure. In short, the counselors receive eight weeks of rigorous experience, and many of the boys make real gains in maturity.

The Division of Gerontology

From the beginning, the Rackham Trustees, carrying out the provisions of Mr. Rackham's will, made grants to various Michigan homes for the aged. Indeed, an early suggestion (1935) from one of the Trustees had been the endowment at the University of "an old folks home." On September 24, 1935, President Ruthven wrote: "As you will recall, I have been asked to get an expert to report to the Trustees of the Horace H. Rackham and Mary A. Rackham Fund on methods of caring for the aged." A laboratory research project related to heredity and aging was subsequently undertaken,[15] but a broad gerontological program did not develop until a number of years later, when the Institute for Human Adjustment became actively interested in work in this field.

On February 9, 1940, Mr. Tibbitts, Director of the Institute, presented to President Ruthven a thirty-four-page proposal for University work with the aged, and in 1943, he became a member of the newly-formed Social Science Research Council's Committee on Social Adjustment of the Aging. The findings of this committee (the first and second reports were published in 1946 and 1948) led to the first official step in the gerontological program at the University: a University Extension course in Problems of Adjustment During Maturity and Old Age, taught by Mr. Tibbitts in the spring of 1948. He developed plans, assisted by Dr. Wilma T. Donahue of the Psychological Clinic, for research into the problems arising from growing old, and in the fall of 1948, through a program of systematic interviews, began to study the actual needs of people over sixty.

These interviews uncovered seven basic needs of the aging: (1) for financial security, (2) for health and physical security, (3) for adequate family and living arrangements, (4) for recognition and status, (5) for activities, (6) for religion, (7) for emotional security. In August, 1949, Mr. Tibbitts left for Washington to become chairman of the Federal Security Agency's Committee on Aging and Geriatrics, and there, as Director of the First National Conference on Aging (August, 1950), he wrote into its program the seven points that had been brought out by the Michigan study. Hence the work done at the very beginning of the University's gerontological activities formed the basis for programs in gerontology throughout the United States.

In 1949 and 1950, Dr. Donahue, as Research Associate in Gerontology, served without title as head of gerontological activities. On June 4, 1951, the Board of Governors formally established the Division of Gerontology as part of the Institute for Human Adjustment, with Dr. Donahue as chairman. The Division remains primarily a research unit, but its educational function is also important. With a permanent staff of only three—although grants for specific research from outside agencies and businesses permit an increase of staff from time to time—the Division conducts courses for the University Extension Service, for the School of Social Work and the School of Education, and for employees in business and industry; it holds short institutes for welfare workers, for Friendly Visitors to the aged, and for workers in old people's homes; it provides advice and counseling for a great many organizations, individuals, and communities. Its list of articles and books indicates an effectiveness reaching well beyond the state of Michigan.

An important aspect of the work in gerontology has been the annual Conference on Aging, beginning in the summer of 1948. At these conferences there are speakers of national reputation, and gerontologists from all parts of the country come to participate in the programs. The proceedings of each of the four conferences have been published and have become standard, basic works in the field of geriatrics. The first three form a unit. They are entitled:

Living Through the Older Years (1949), *Planning the Older Years* (1950), and *Growing in the Older Years* (1951). *Rehabilitation of the Older Worker* (1952)[16] is the title of the proceedings of the fourth Annual Conference.

Two examples will indicate something of the Division's work in the field. Throughout 1951, assisted in part by grants from the Joseph E. Gordon Foundation and the Altrusa Society of Detroit, the Division conducted a study of the effects of organized activities on the residents in homes for the aged. In homes where the programs were tried, sociability was greatly enhanced; in homes not using the programs, the natural withdrawal and isolation of old people increased with the passage of time. Another example is the Division's Forum on Aging, held June 5, 1953, in Grand Rapids, after a year's introductory work. Assisted by Grand Rapids agencies and the University's Extension Service, the Division led the Forum to investigate changes desirable for old people in their community and action old people can take to bring these changes about. The elder citizens of Grand Rapids were aided in discovering and analyzing their own problems, and by working for the desired civic changes, found themselves once more moving toward integration into community life.

The Division's support comes from the Horace H. Rackham Fund, from research grants from outside the University, and from the University for teaching services in various departments.

This account of the work of the five units is also an account of the Institute for Human Adjustment as it operates today; it engages in no activities other than those centered in the individual units. Their various fields cover the large areas of social service designated by Mrs. Rackham and by Mr. Rackham's will, and they are sufficiently flexible to shift their emphases with changing conditions. While they receive part of their money from interested outside sources and from the University for services rendered to students and for the teaching services of their staff members, they all received early support and encouragement from the Rackham Trustees or from the Board of Governors of the Horace H. Rackham School of Graduate Studies, and at present they are receiving support from one or another of the Rackham endowments. They have all demonstrated their effectiveness in translating the results of scholarly research into service to the public at large and, in so doing, have strengthened the ties between the University and the people of the state which supports it.

The Rackham Arthritis Research Unit

On May 12, 1937, Dean A. C. Furstenberg, of the Medical School, outlined for President Ruthven and the Board of Governors of the Horace H. Rackham School of Graduate Studies a plan for research in arthritis, requesting $10,000 a year for five years. The need for such research was clear. Rheumatic diseases were then, as they are still, one of the major challenges to the medical profession and one of the major causes of public concern, for rheumatism is the most prevalent of chronic diseases. In 1937 the United States Public Health Service found that nearly seven million persons in the country were disabled by rheumatism in its various forms—nearly half of them by rheumatoid arthritis— and that it ranked second only to nervous and mental diseases as a reason for chronic invalidism. Most frequently crippling of all diseases, but seldom fatal, it led the chronic diseases in its social and economic importance. At the same time, there was little knowledge of its causes, treatment was largely empirical, and nothing was known of preventive measures. Few, if any, research centers for the study of rheumatic diseases existed, and the nature of the disease processes and the structures they affect was little understood.

The Board of Governors recognized research in arthritis as desirable and as offering real possibilities for the alleviation of human suffering, specified by Mr. Rackham's will as one of his objectives. Upon approval by the Board, Dean Furstenberg appointed a committee to guide the project: Doctors Cyrus C. Sturgis, Chairman of the Department of Internal Medicine; Harley A. Haynes, Director of the University Hospital; and Carl E. Badgley, Professor of Surgery. Dr. Richard H. Freyberg, who was first in his medical-school class of 1930 and had been a member of the hospital staff from that date, was appointed to supervise the clinic. Dr. Freyberg visited arthritis clinics in New York, Boston, Philadelphia, and Rochester (Minnesota) during the summer and fall and began his research on January 1, 1938.

In the meantime (June 18, 1937), the Trustees of the Horace H. Rackham and Mary A. Rackham Fund had decided to give $1,000,000 to establish the Rackham Arthritis Research Fund for a Unit in the University Hospital devoted to "the prevention, cure and mitigation of arthritis," and the Board of Governors had agreed that the $10,000 they had granted should be returned to the Horace H. Rackham Fund. The Trustees provided that the Unit should continue for five years, and then from year to year, if approved by the Board of Governors; the income from the Fund could be applied to other major research if and when the Unit went out of existence; after fifteen years the endowment and its increase could be added to the original $4,000,000 which had become the Horace H. Rackham Fund. These provisions, however, have so far proved unnecessary, and, in fact, the recognition of the need for research in this field has increased. A study by the National Research Council in 1948 revealed that the total support for arthritis research amounted to only $200,000 a year and that the Rackham Arthritis Research Unit was one of the three major research units in the country studying the disease.

In 1944, Dr. William D. Robinson was placed in charge of the Unit, succeeding Dr. Freyberg, and he was succeeded, in 1953, by Dr. Ivan F. Duff. By April, 1946, the Unit had issued thirty-seven articles and books and was gaining widespread recognition, so wide, indeed, that, at present, outside support exceeds that from the Rackham endowment.[17] The Unit has treated hundreds of arthritic patients and has conducted extensive research. While most of the discoveries concerning this widespread and evasive disease have so far been negative, they have made a significant contribution by clearing away a great many mistaken theories as to its cause and treatment.

It was found, for example, that there seems to be no connection between arthritis and metabolism, that it is not infectious or of bacteriological background, and that it is not caused by vitamin deficiencies. The hereditary nature of gout was established by research carried on by the Unit in co-operation with Dr. C. W. Cotterman of the University's Heredity Clinic. Improvements in the use of gold salts in the treatment of rheumatoid arthritis and a better recognition of the cases in which they could help have resulted from the Unit's work. That X-ray treatment will halt the progress of most early cases of rheumatoid arthritis of the spine, although it has little effect in the more advanced cases or in involvements of other joints, has been demonstrated.

In 1949, shortly after the development of ACTH and cortisone, the Unit began an intensive study of the use of these new drugs in rheumatoid arthritis. Three years of careful study of a group of patients confirmed early findings that these drugs are suppressive of arthritic symptoms, not curative, and that for only relatively few patients can a dosage be found which can be continued for long periods of time and produce worthwhile alleviation of the disease symptoms, without, at the same time, producing an undesirable degree of hyperadrenalism.

More recently, attention has been centered on improving the knowledge of the tissue primarily involved in these diseases—the connective tissue. Research on its chemistry and physiology, always an interest of the Unit, has been intensified by the addition of new staff members experienced in these fields. Along with this work will go studies of the joint fluid which, with the connective tissue, is the site of the earliest pathological conditions in rheumatism. With better knowledge in these areas should come greater possibilities for success in the prevention and cure of the arthritic diseases. Dr. Sturgis believes that this approach may prove to be the most productive yet tried.

The Fenton Community Center

When the five Trustees of the Rackham estate were considering the projects they should support in carrying out the provisions and intent of Mr. Rackham's will, the establishment of a community center in a small community seemed to them appropriate and desirable, and as four of them knew the Fenton community well, its interests and its needs, Fenton was chosen for the undertaking.

Of the five Trustees, the three members of the Horton family, Mrs. Rackham, Mrs. Bussey, and Mr. Horton,[18] had been born in Fenton; and another, Mr. Rolland, had grown up there. Mr. Rackham had known and loved the town. In the account of their various grants and endowments, the *Horace H. Rackham and Mary A. Rackham Fund,* published by the Trustees in 1940, Fenton was described as "a decorous, tree-shaded, typically American village in the heart of an agricultural district . . . without a central gathering place" and with "no community facilities for the promotion of leadership, educational advancement, social enjoyment, or civic improvement." The population numbered around four thousand.

In 1919, in the center of town, along the Shiawasee River, the Hortons had established and presented to the village of Fenton the Dexter Horton Park, on what had been part of their father's land, and they proposed that the community center be located on adjoining land. Accordingly, on January 20, 1937, the Trustees created a $200,000 trust fund to be used by Fenton to buy and clear the land and build a community house, any remaining balance to supply income for upkeep. Since clearing the land would involve tearing down the old Firemen's Hall that contained the city offices, a new building for the purpose had to be provided, and the Trustees made an additional appropriation of $5,000 toward its construction. The highly prized town clock, then nearly seventy-five years old, was to be transferred from the old building to the new City and Fire Hall.

Plans for the Community Center building proceeded. It was designed by Eliel Saarinen, who had designed all of the buildings of the Cranbrook Foundation, at Bloomfield Hills, and his son Eero. It was built by the W. E. Wood Company and was landscaped according to the plans of the landscape artist, Mrs. F. W. Whittlesey, of Phoenix, Arizona, daughter of Mr. Horton. The Trustees formally presented the building to the Village of Fenton on the afternoon of October 3, 1938, with President Ruthven addressing the audience of five hundred in the auditorium-ballroom on the second floor.

Because most of the original $200,000 trust fund had been used for the land, building, and landscaping, the Trustees added $100,000 as an endowment for upkeep, and again, on December 2, 1938, they added $35,000 to the endowment, along with a gift of $4,425 for initial expenses. On January 26, 1940, there was a final gift of $10,000 for capital improvements. The total endowment, then, amounted to $135,000, and outright gifts for land, building, and expenses totaled $219,425.

On July 29, 1938, an agreement was signed between the Horace H. Rackham and Mary A. Rackham Fund, as donor, the Regents of the University of Michigan, as donee, and the Village of Fenton, as beneficiary, vesting in the Regents control over the management and investment of the endowment fund of the Fenton Community Center, which was to be "commingled with the principal of the Endowment Fund of the Horace H. Rackham School of Graduate Studies," with a proportionate share of the income to be paid to the Board of Governors of the Fenton Community Center. The University receives no income from the Fund for its own use.

The composition and function of the Board of Governors of the Center was defined by the agreement between the three interested parties and remains unchanged. It is composed of seven members, serving without compensation, and includes the President of the Village of Fenton and the Superintendent of Schools. It manages and directs the income and appoints the Director of the Center, but the Board of Governors of the Horace H. Rackham School of Graduate Studies must approve this appointment. The Director arranges and supervises the program of activities, which are planned, as stated in the agreement, to secure "the enthusiastic co-operation of local groups, and have as their objectives the development of leadership and the benefiting of the people of the community in the fields of health, recreation, morals, cultural development and civic improvement. It is the expectation and desire . . . . that the Community Center Board of Governors and the Director will endeavor to co-operate with the Horace H. Rackham School of Graduate Studies of the University of Michigan to the end that the Community Center shall at all times have the benefit of the expert counsel of those members of the faculty of the University of Michigan especially trained in community-center activities."

The Center's Board of Governors is a self-perpetuating body, made up entirely of residents of Fenton and the immediately surrounding rural area. Each year it submits a report and financial statement to the University and publishes its financial report in a local newspaper. The income from the Fenton Community Center Fund, together with that derived from local money-raising activities, gifts, and fees charged organizations for the use of the building, determines the size of the budget within which the Center must operate.

This arrangement has been remarkably successful. The Board of Governors and the Director by prudent management of expenditures have been able to maintain the building in good condition, institute some improvements, build up a substantial carry-over in the bank balance, and finance a well-planned, comprehensive, and flexible program of activities and of co-operative undertakings with the school and with local groups.

In July, 1948, as Mr. Russell D. Haddon was completing his last year before resigning as Director, he issued a report outlining the Center's activities during its first ten years of existence and noted that for the year 1947–48, 1,291 meetings had been held in the building, with a total attendance of 59,021. In the list were small club and committee meetings and large public meetings, dances sponsored by the Center and by private organizations, public school events, nursery school sessions, and adult education classes.

Fully as inclusive of the community needs and interests has been the program carried on under Mr. N. H. Chesnut, who, in September, 1948, succeeded Mr. Haddon as Director. In his report for 1952–53, Mr. Chesnut summarized the use made of the building:

> In all, some part of the building was used 1,162 times during the past year. Of these meetings, 668 were adult groups and 494 were meetings of those of high school age or younger. Because it is necessary to obtain additional income to pay running expenses, a large number of these groups pay a small rental, but it is interesting to note that the number of paying groups was just slightly larger than the free groups, and that there were nearly as many youth groups as adult. Over 50,000 people attended these meetings during the year, and several thousand more visited the Center during the year to obtain information or to participate in some of the services that the Center affords.

These services include a loan closet of furniture and equipment for the sick room, with, among other things, hospital beds, wheel chairs, and crutches of practically all sizes. These articles are loaned for a limited time, free of charge, but, for the more expensive ones, a refundable deposit is required to ensure their return in good condition.

By providing temporary headquarters, as needed, for visiting representatives of certain state and federal agencies, the Center saves the local residents the inconvenience and expense of traveling to the permanent headquarters in Flint, or elsewhere, for interviews. This service is of particular help to those who must consult the Bureau of Social Aid regarding Old Age Assistance, or the Social Security Administration regarding Old Age Pensions.

The Michigan Children's Institute makes use of the Center for bringing together children who are ready for adoption and those who wish to adopt them. A representative of the Institute brings the child to the Center a day or two before the meeting, where "a room is provided so that the child may become accustomed to the surroundings. Then the prospective parents come to spend some time with the child, and if everything is satisfactory, the child is taken to their home and later the adoption may follow. Twelve children have been placed in homes this year."

The County Mobile X-ray Unit was accommodated in the Center's grounds, and for a fee of $1.00, chest X rays were given to adults and to the children who did not get them free at the school. The American Red Cross twice sent Blood Bank units to the Center from Lansing. Local women registered those who came to donate blood and also prepared the food that was given to those who participated. The amount of blood secured was 325 pints.

The Employment Service was continued, although high employment reduced the number of requests, and for the most part, they were for housework, baby sitting, and odd jobs. The use of this service naturally fluctuates widely with general conditions of employment.

Voting at national, state, county, and township elections takes place at the Center, as well as caucuses for village elections. Seven denominational churches used the Center during the year, two of them conducting all of their religious services there. Six lodges and service clubs met there regularly.

Old-time and modern dances were sponsored by civic groups and were very popular. All of the proceeds were turned over to the Center and made a substantial addition to its funds.

Adult Education classes, though not so numerous as in the early years, were still an important activity. Some were organized and promoted by the Center and then turned over to the school for teaching; for these a small fee was charged. They included typing, furniture refinishing, sewing for beginners, and rug making. Classes at the Center were free; they included a cardiac homemaker's class, a nurse's training class, two mothercraft classes, and the high school Bible class.

For five years the Center has sponsored a "Golden Age Group." During 1952–53 many people in the community furnished music and entertainment, and a service club volunteered to meet any deficit. The report stated ". . . good-sized crowds have turned out to the meetings, which are held every two weeks during the year. About 100 people come to these meetings to enjoy the lunch provided and the programs, consisting of dancing, cards, music, movies, and occasionally a speaker. The members have to be at least 55 years of age to join, and over 300 have joined to date. Potlucks are held occasionally and at least one picnic is held each year."

This report of the Director confirms the impression left by earlier reports, that the Center has become, as the Trustees had hoped it would, a focal point for the life of the village. The list of the groups participating in the Center's program or making use of its facilities includes a large proportion of the civic, religious, and recreational activities of the community. It has set a pattern for such centers that has proved practical and popular, and its success testifies to the foresight that led to its establishment.

The Horace H. Rackham Educational Memorial

In the late 1920's, the Detroit Engineering Society began planning an addition to its quarters. When the Rackham Fund came into being, Mr. E. J. Burdick, Mr. Harold S. Ellington (who, with Mr. Alvin E. Harley, eventually designed the building), and Mr. John H. Hunt, "joining into a committee to further the interests of the Society, met frequently with the trustees of the Horace H. Rackham and Mary A. Rackham Fund, discussing conditions under which it would be possible for Detroit technical men to receive substantial aid from the Fund and for the Fund to carry out to the fullest extent in this connection the wishes of its founder," and decided that a "review of the aims and past activities of the Detroit Engineering Society indicated that its purposes were identical with many of those for which the Horace H. Rackham and Mary A. Rackham Fund was established . . . ."[19]

In April, 1936, the Society reincorporated itself as the Engineering Society of Detroit, one of its aims being to provide, through a common meeting place, "a continuing process of education for our younger engineers." The Society had earlier set forth the following educational aims:

1) to provide public education in engineering matters
2) to encourage research into engineering problems of public interest
3) to "provide assistance to industry, particularly the smaller industries unable to maintain continuously adequate engineering staffs, by supplying library service, and employment service supplying technically qualified men . . . ."
4) to "cooperate with educational institutions by investigating candidates for scholarships and fellowships in engineering and applied science, and supporting scholarships, special instruction, or research."[20]

On March 17, 1936, the Trustees gave the Engineering Society $500,000, creating the Rackham Engineering Foundation—in effect, a special committee of Engineers—to administer the money, in trust, for the Society. Early in 1937, the Rackham Trustees gave a second $500,000, and later in the year, Mrs. Rackham added a like amount, making the total $1,500,000. Plans for a suitable building and location were, however, slow in getting under way. At this time, Dr. James D. Bruce, Vice-President of the University in charge of University Relations, which included the extension program, was urging President Ruthven to find a permanent, central building for the scattered extension classes in Detroit. Mr. Bryson D. Horton, as a member of the Engineering Society and as one of the Trustees, provided the link between the Society's projected building and the University's needs.[21]

President Ruthven knew of property in the center of Detroit, facing the Detroit Institute of Arts and the Public Library, which he believed alumnus

Dexter M. Ferry, Jr., would sell to the University at a moderate figure. It was clear that a jointly owned building on this property would benefit both parties and the city of Detroit; for neither the University nor the Engineering Society could afford, singly, the general facilities they could build together, and Detroit would gain a gracious building to accompany its Library and Institute of Arts.

After some discussion as to whether to erect two buildings on common grounds or to share a single structure, the University and the Engineering Society of Detroit adopted President Ruthven's plan for a central auditorium and banquet hall flanked by two equal wings. It was decided that the Society would have one wing and the University would have the other wing and the central part: in other words, two-thirds of the land and building would be the property of the University and one-third would belong to the Engineering Society, and the money invested by each in the joint project was to be in about that proportion. Later, on August 18, 1939, the Society and the University signed an agreement concerning the costs to the Society for the use of the auditorium and banquet hall on the University's side of the building.

On March 27, 1939, the Regents accepted an anonymous $500,000 to be used for a "Horace H. Rackham School of Graduate Studies, Detroit Branch . . . adjacent to, near to or adjoining the building to be constructed by the Rackham Engineering Foundation . . . for the benefit of the Engineering Society of Detroit." The University's building was to be used for extension courses, adult and undergraduate, and for "younger professional men who may wish to improve themselves in their chosen line of work." This anonymous gift came from Mrs. Rackham. She further specified, in line with the agreement which had covered the gift for the Horace H. Rackham School of Graduate Studies in Ann Arbor, that the University "maintain said building in first-class condition at all times," and, further, that the $500,000 would be withdrawn unless the Trustees, by June 30, added at least another $200,000 from the Horace H. Rackham and Mary A. Rackham Fund. On May 11 the Trustees gave the University $500,000 toward the building.

Plans were approved November 11, 1939, but again Mrs. Rackham felt that more land was needed to give the building an attractive setting. On January 29, 1940, she sent a letter to the University and the Engineering Society giving them, jointly, $750,000 for the other (southern) half of the block and for landscaping, and the building plans were then adjusted to the enlarged site. Harley and Ellington, the architects, had harmonized the quite diverse requirements of the two prospective occupants and secured the approval of two rather complicated organizations forty miles apart. In charge for the University, as for the Ann Arbor building, were Mr. John C. Christensen, Controller, and Professor Lewis M. Gram, Director of Plant Extension. The W. E. Wood Company broke ground July 1, 1940. The cornerstone was laid on

December 20, 1940, and the Horace H. Rackham Educational Memorial was presented by the Trustees to its joint owners on Wednesday, January 28, 1942. The total bill from the W. E. Wood Company was $1,297,246.66, about $17,500 below their guarantee.[22] The building and land cost the Engineering Society $710,000, and the University, $1,244,000; the University put the balance of its $1,500,000 into a reserve fund for equipment.

The building is in constant use and is perhaps the finest single gift to adult education in the United States. In comparison with the Ann Arbor building, it is a smaller, but equally beautiful memorial. The exterior of white Georgia marble with spandrels of dark granite midway up the tall, bronze-framed windows is striking. Marshall Fredericks, Cranbrook Academy of Art, decorated the façades with sculptured groups, and Zoltan Sepeshy, also of Cranbrook, painted the murals. The central part, taller than the wings, houses banquet hall, kitchens, and furnace rooms on the ground floor, and, on the main floor, an auditorium with 1,000 seats, and a stage on which the engineers (with University permission) can, if they wish, drive a truck. The University wing contains Extension Service Offices, classrooms, lecture rooms, library, lounge, and broadcasting studio. The Engineering wing contains offices, lounges, committee rooms, playrooms, library, small auditorium (300 seats), dining room, and another kitchen.

The University's part of the building is the headquarters for the class and field work carried on in Detroit by the School of Social Work, which maintains an office there. Forty-three students, last year, were regularly enrolled in this Detroit program, which parallels the work given in Ann Arbor for the first year of the two-year program leading to the University's degree of Master of Social Work.

The University's greatest use of the building, however, is by its Extension Service. In 1952–53, 249 courses were offered, and there were 7,334 individual course enrollments, 2,563 of which were for University credit. Of the enrollments for credit, 1,327 were by graduate students taking advantage of the opportunity offered by the Center for Graduate Study to earn credit toward the master's degree. At the Center, which is maintained in the building with the co-operation of the Extension Service, and at four other Centers for Graduate Study throughout the state, students may complete most of the work for the master's degree in evening classes. An increasing number of students, particularly teachers in the public schools, are availing themselves of this opportunity.

In his report to the President of the University for 1951–52, Everett J. Soop, the Director of the Extension Service, noted:

In November, 1951, the Extension Service brought to Detroit the traveling exhibit on atomic energy which was prepared by the American Museum of Atomic Energy at Oak Ridge, Tennessee .... Nearly 22,000 persons visited the exhibit during the week it was on display in the Rackham Building . . . . Many schools and colleges made arrangements to have their students attend in groups.

The class program has always been the major activity of the Detroit Extension Center, and this year was no exception . . . . There are always a few results of innovations to be mentioned. For example, the expansion of the Business Administration program from 11 to 27 courses produced a corresponding increase in enrollments from 318 to 807. Also there has been a steady increase in the number of doctoral candidates who enroll in special foreign language reading courses . . . .

A special program and open house on February 26, 1952, celebrated the tenth anniversary of extension activities in the Horace H. Rackham Educational Memorial. Honored guests were President Emeritus Alexander G. Ruthven and Dr. Harvey M. Merker. At the time of its dedication, Dr. Ruthven had accepted the building for the Board of Regents and Dr. Merker, for the Engineering Society of Detroit, of which he was then president. Other participants were Professor Wesley Maurer, representing the instructors who had taught continuously in the program since the opening of the building, several student representatives, and the Extension symphony orchestra and choir.

Two unusual features of the year at the Detroit Center were an exhibit of paintings and etchings by Wilfred B. Shaw, Director Emeritus of Alumni Relations, and another of paintings by two University artists, Gerome Kamrowski and Edith Dines (Mrs. Kamrowski). The student activity program continued to grow, with the result that the informality of the coffee hours and the opportunities for students to talk with one another and with their instructors have done much to weld heterogeneous groups into a student body characterized by a spirit of friendliness and co-operation. The auditorium and other facilities of the Rackham Building were used during the year by seven campus departments and thirty-eight Detroit organizations.

These highlights of one year's activities indicate the diverse needs and interests of Detroit's adult population that the University is serving through the facilities provided by the Horace H. Rackham Educational Memorial.

Rackham Fellowships and Scholarships

Graduate fellowships and undergraduate scholarships were an important interest of the Trustees of the Horace H. Rackham and Mary A. Rackham Fund, and they early set aside money for these purposes.

The Rackham Graduate Fellowships

When, on April 27, 1936, the Board of Governors of the new Horace H. Rackham School of Graduate Studies met for the first time and made an appropriation for graduate fellowships, a number of Rackham Fellowships had already been awarded by specific grants from the Rackham Trustees. On November 2, 1934, from $12,000 granted for the study of juvenile delinquency, Mrs. Minna Faust had received the first fellowship supported by Rackham money: the Michigan Juvenile Delinquency Information Service Fellowship, with a stipend of $500. The Trustees had also designated $10,000 for ten Rackham Fellowships, and the Regents had accepted this gift on August 31, 1934, at a special meeting. There proved to be not enough time, however, to find ten suitable candidates before the opening of the fall semester, but for the second semester it was possible to appoint ten Special Predoctoral Fellows, at $500 each. Then, for the year 1935–36, seven $1,000 Rackham Research Fellowships were awarded from the Trustees' grant of the previous year and an additional grant of $3,500 in 1935. The Board of Governors, at its first meeting, voted to continue, at $1,000 each, the ten fellowships originally designated by the Trustees and to add two postdoctoral fellowships, at $2,000 each. The Board has continued these twelve fellowships each year.

On May 19, 1947, the stipend for the two postdoctoral fellowships was increased by $500 each, and on November 28, 1947 (for the year 1948–49), the stipend for the ten predoctorals was raised to $1,500, making "these Fellowships, as was originally intended, the most attractive fellowships in the Graduate School."[23] In December, 1951, the stipend for the postdoctorals (for the year 1952–53) was advanced to $3,000, and the following year, because of "increasing cost of living" and the "increased stipend of similar fellowships," the predoctoral stipend was raised to $1,750 for the year 1953–54.

In the fall of 1945 (confirmed May 20, 1946), the Board of Governors set aside a fund of $30,000 for a third category of fellowships: the Horace H. Rackham Special Fellowships for exceptionally promising graduate students whose graduate studies were interrupted by the war. The need for these has naturally diminished with the passage of time, and for the present year (1953–54) only $10,000 was appropriated.

Since the fall of 1936, thirty-one Rackham Postdoctoral Fellowships and 166 Rackham Predoctoral Fellowships have been awarded to 156 people, at a total expenditure for the postdoctorals of $65,250, and for the predoctorals of $169,132.26. No person has held fellowships for more than three years. Since the fall of 1946, 95 Rackham Special Fellowships have been awarded to 86 persons (none of whom has received grants from the other two fellowship funds) at a total expenditure of $77,820. The selection standards were somewhat liberalized for this group, and their success has not been so conspicuous as that of the other Rackham Fellows, who, consistently, have been among the best scholars in the Graduate School.

Of the 242 Rackham Fellows in all three categories, grouped by departments in Table I, 177 have received the Ph.D. degree. Many of them are now serving on college faculties in this country and abroad. One is an economist in Bombay; one, a professor of engineering mechanics in the University of the Philippines; one, a physicist in China; one, a political scientist in the United Nations educational program for Asia and the Far East, with offices in Paruskawan Palace, Bangkok. In this country, Dr. Mark W. Bills is now Superintendent of Schools in Kansas City. Dr. Kenneth Millar, a Coleridge scholar, better known as a writer of detective stories under the name of John Ross MacDonald, lectured at the University during the Popular Arts Symposium (summer, 1953) on trends and values in detective fiction. Dr. Chad Walsh, who was awarded a Rackham Fellowship for three successive years and who took his Ph.D. in the linguistics of Early Middle English, is now a highly regarded poet, professor, theological writer, and editor of *The Beloit Poetry Journal*.

Twenty-one former Rackham Fellows teach and carry on research in twelve different departments of the University of Michigan. Among these Assistant Professor Hugh Z. Norton has staged a large number of plays in the Department of Speech, and serves as dramatics editor for the *Quarterly Journal of Speech*. Assistant Professor Robert W. Pidd has contributed significantly to the development of the Physics Department's synchrotron. Dr. Robert R. White, Professor of Chemical and Metallurgical Engineering, is a member of the Executive Board of the Horace H. Rackham School of Graduate Studies. Articles and books written by this group include those of Professor Gardner Ackley on prices and economic theory, those of Professor Allen P. Britton on early American music, those of Assistant Professor Robert F. Haugh on the English and American novel, and those of Assistant Professor Lila Miller on the biochemistry of digestion and secretion. One of the most prolific writers among former Rackham Fellows on the University faculty is Associate Professor Arthur W. Burks, of the Department of Philosophy, whose studies in logic and empiricism have led him to an analysis of the circuits and the theory of large electronic computing machines, as well as to Lewis Carroll and to a "Theory of Proper Names." Another is Dr. Andrew J. Berger, Instructor in

Anatomy, an ornithologist and editor, who has written extensively on the bird population of Michigan and bird nesting habits.

TABLE I

Graduate Students Awarded Rackham Fellowships in Various Fields 1936–53

Anthropology	5	Geology	5
Astronomy	3	German	6
Bacteriology	1	History	11
Botany	19	Mathematics	20
Business Administration	1	Near Eastern Studies	1
Ceramic Archeology	1	Oriental Studies	2
Chemistry	25	Philosophy	5
Classical Studies	4	Physics	24
Economics	9	Psychology	11
Education	13	Political Science	4
Engineering	14	Romance Languages	8
English	12	Sociology	2
Fine Arts	2	Speech	5
Forestry	4	Zoology	21
Geography	4		

The Horace H. Rackham Undergraduate Scholarships

On February 28, 1938, a little more than three years after beginning their support of graduate fellowships, the Trustees of the Rackham Estate gave the University $100,000 to be known as the Horace H. Rackham Fund for Undergraduate Scholarships. This fund is separate from the loan fund of $100,000 left to the University by Mr. Rackham's will and is administered by a small committee of which the Dean of the Graduate School is chairman. President Ruthven, then on a committee for the Rhodes Scholarships, drew up similar requirements for the Rackham Undergraduate Scholarships: (1) high scholastic standing, (2) moral character, (3) leadership, (4) vigor and physical ability. The stipend is $500. In general, these scholarships are awarded to entering first-year students and are renewable for each succeeding year of the four-year undergraduate program if the student's record meets the requirements. On the average, awards are made to two entering students a year. Including the school year 1953–54, the fund has assisted twenty-eight scholars. Eight were athletes, and all were active on campus. About a third became members of Phi Beta Kappa. Nearly a third are now engineers, but the majority are junior business and industrial executives; among the rest are a few doctors, a few lawyers, one forester, one historian, and one classics scholar.

Rackham Research Grants and Publication Grants

Mr. Rackham's will had listed support of "study, research, and publication" among the responsibilities of the Trustees of the Horace H. Rackham and Mary A. Rackham Fund, and as early as 1934, they were financing specific research studies at the University of Michigan and at other institutions. At that time, the Graduate School, of course, was supporting a research program, but it was, necessarily, a limited one. On March 25, 1921, the Regents had approved a proposal by Dean Alfred H. Lloyd, of the Graduate School, "for facilitating research and improving teaching in all departments of the University." Dean Lloyd's proposal clearly formulates the rationale for all subsequent faculty research, including that currently supported by the income from the Rackham endowments:

> Not only are research and teaching essential to a vigorous and efficient university education; also, they are essential to each other. Without this constant association and interchange education must lose vitality. A university that includes among its teachers competent investigators and original thinkers without providing them with adequate opportunity for research and investigation is failing seriously in one of its primary purposes.

Approving Dean Lloyd's proposal on September 24, 1925, the Regents had established, with $3,000 transferred from funds held in trust, a "special Research Trust Fund," and in the fall of 1927 it was enlarged by $30,000 from the University general funds and became, as it still is, the Faculty Research Fund. It has been to supplement this Fund (now $50,000 per year), and the grants for research which have come to the University from government, industry, and private sources, that a considerable part of the income from the Horace H. Rackham Fund has been used.

The original $4,000,000 in this Fund was later augmented in several ways, and the *Financial Report* of the University for June 30, 1953, shows the principal to be $4,578,012.02. The income, except for that from the $400,000 earmarked for the Institute for Human Adjustment (noted earlier), provides the money for the Rackham Predoctoral, Postdoctoral, and Special Fellowships, the Rackham Faculty Research Grants, the Rackham Publication Grants, and certain small, authorized expenditures. As a preliminary to an account of the research supported by this endowment, one of the most significant research grants received by any university, it will perhaps be well to outline the early research grants of the Rackham Trustees.

Their first grants for research, three in number, were made in 1934, including one of $15,000, with an additional $5,000 in 1935, for the support of Dr.

36

Horace H. Rackham School of Graduate Studies

Russell W. Bunting's investigation of dental caries in children,[24] which he had been pursuing for some years. The Board of Governors of the Horace H. Rackham School of Graduate Studies, when it came into being, continued to support Dr. Bunting's project through the fiscal year 1937–38, making two grants of $9,500 each, and bringing to $39,000 the total contribution of Rackham funds to this project. With these grants, Dr. Bunting made basic investigations of the relationship between tooth decay and fluorine, publishing more than three dozen articles and a monograph on dentistry and dental caries and becoming an authority in the field.[25] Assisted by grants totaling $7,996.30 (1940–43), Dr. Philip Jay continued Dr. Bunting's research into the causes of tooth decay.

Another of the three original grants by the Trustees was one for $12,000 for research by the Bureau of Reference and Research in Government, into the problems of government, particularly in Michigan; support for this project was continued by a second grant of $12,000 in 1935, and by $12,000 from the Board of Governors for 1936–37, the total amounting to $36,000. Although the Bureau was one of the oldest organizations in this country devoted to governmental research, the small appropriations that had hitherto been available had been used chiefly in developing a library for students in municipal administration. The Rackham grant made possible a significant expansion of its research activities, as is evidenced by the issuance of a number of bulletins and pamphlets on governmental problems in Michigan. Mr. Harold D. Smith, Director of the Bureau beginning July 1, 1934, published *Tax Limitation in Michigan*,[26] and edited the *Michigan Municipal Review*. When Mr. Smith left Ann Arbor in 1937 to become Budget Director of the state of Michigan, and subsequently, to become Director of the Federal Budget, in Washington, he was succeeded by Robert S. Ford, Professor of Economics. Professor Ford served as Director until his appointment as Assistant Dean of the Horace H. Rackham School of Graduate Studies in 1950. In 1936 the Bureau of Reference and Research in Government (now the Bureau of Government) had become a part of the Graduate School's Institute of Public Administration, supported by the general funds of the University.

The results of the third early grant—$5,000 for a study of juvenile delinquency in 1934, followed by an additional $7,000 in 1935—have been detailed earlier.

In 1934, 1935, and 1936 the Trustees made a number of other grants to the University for specific research projects, which, together with those already mentioned, are listed in Table II. The range of the subjects covered reflects the Trustees' understanding of the broad scope of Mr. Rackham's interests and intentions and their own appreciation of the importance of research, not only for practical applications of basic principles but for the extension of knowledge.

TABLE II
Faculty Research Grants by the Trustees of the
Horace H. Rackham and Mary A. Rackham Fund
1934 – 1936

1934

For astronomy in South Africa	$ 6,000.00
For research into cancer of the eye (Dr. Laura A. Lane)	2,500.00
For research at the University Heart Station (Dr. Frank N. Wilson)	5,000.00

1934 and 1935

For excavations in Egypt	50,000.00
For research into juvenile delinquency (Professor Lowell J. Carr)	12,000.00
For research into dental caries (Dr. Russell W. Bunting)	20,000.00
For research by the Bureau of Reference and Research in Government	24,000.00
For research into brain psychology (Dr. Norman R. F. Maier)	4,481.85
For research into metabolism (Dr. Louis H. Newburgh)	6,200.00

1935

For research into infantile paralysis	5,000.00
For research into rickets (Dr. Coral A. Lilly)	1,500.00
For Michigan Indian history (Dr. Carl E. Guthe and Dr. Wilbert B. Hinsdale)	10,000.00
For research in surgery (Dr. Frederick A. Coller)	3,800.00
For research at the Fresh Air Camp into juvenile delinquency (Professor Lowell J. Carr)	18,000.00
For research into visual acuity (Professors Carl R. Brown and Burton D. Thuma)	1,400.00
For nuclear research and the building of a cyclotron (Professor Harrison M. Randall)	25,000.00

1935 and 1936

For construction of a solar tower at the McMath-Hulbert Observatory, Lake Angelus, Michigan	25,000.00
Total	$219,881.85

Two of the projects reached completion without further support. On May 18, 1934, the Trustees had given the University $20,000 to build a therapeutic swimming pool for the victims of infantile paralysis. When, in 1935, they added $5,000 for treatment and research, the University Hospital established a new Physical Therapy Unit. By February 28, 1936, only $1,000 of this latter grant had been used, and Dean Furstenberg received permission from the Trustees to transfer the remaining $4,000 to the $15,000 fund which they had given for hospitalization of needy expectant mothers. The following April, President Franklin D. Roosevelt's Birthday Ball Commission established a new Infantile Paralysis Research fund of $1,000, under the directorship of Dr. Max M. Peet, and the Therapeutic Pool and the Physical Therapy Unit then became integral parts of the Hospital. Dr. Coral A. Lilly obtained conclusive results in his study of rickets and the Vitamin D in common foods within a year after receiving his Rackham grant of $1,500 (July 31, 1935). On March 17, 1936, Dr. Lilly reported that experiments with albino rats indicated beyond a doubt that common foods "contain enough Vitamin D to *produce normal bone and prevent rickets*," to cure even extreme rickets, and to operate "better than do standard preparations of Vitamin D . . . the universal teaching that it is necessary to add cod liver oil, halibut liver oil or irradiated substances to common food diets is erroneous."

Support for continuing the remainder of the research projects begun by grants from the Rackham Trustees was voted by the Board of Governors of the Horace H. Rackham School of Graduate Studies at its first meeting, in April, 1936, and from that time all new requests from University staff members were referred, not to the Trustees, but to the Board. At its second meeting, in May, 1936, the Board made its first grants in response to these new requests: one for a field study of commuting between Detroit and Windsor, one for laboratory work on fossil fauna from Mexico, one for the expenses of the Institute of Archaeology, and one to assist in the completion of a five-volume report on the United States Commerce Commission. Already the Board was indicating its intention of following the policy established by Mr. Rackham during his lifetime, reaffirmed by his will, and continued by the Trustees: to support basic and applied research in all fields, and the publication of its results.

The six categories under which Rackham research grants are listed are: Physical Sciences, Biological Sciences, Language and Literature, Social Sciences, Fine Arts, Health Sciences.[27] The individual grants in these subjects will be found in Appendix III.

Physical Sciences

The physical scientist, in seeking to measure and weigh the universe and to make its forces useful, needs elaborate and costly instruments. It is not surprising, therefore, that grants in this field from the Horace H. Rackham Fund have exceeded those in any other, totaling $366,870.25. The several grants for the maintenance and operation of the cyclotron constitute the largest amount given for a single project; the second largest was for the purchase and operation of an electron microscope. Significant contributions were also made to the University's astronomical observatories. Some of the grants in the physical sciences will be described here, under headings arranged according to the amount of support for each field, in ascending order.

Mineralogy

Professor E. William Heinrich is the only mineralogist to have applied for a Rackham research grant. As a member of the United States Geological Sur-

vey and, later, as a member of the University of Michigan faculty, Dr. Heinrich had studied the composition of pegmatites—varieties of granites—at various places in this country. He had developed techniques for assaying and
mapping deposits of this valuable stone, a primary source of sheet-mica, feld-
spar, beryl, tantalum, columbium, lithium, and rare earth elements. On December 5, 1949, Dr. Heinrich received a $1,510 Rackham grant to study the
pegmatites of Norway, Sweden, Finland, and Germany, which had been
neither mapped nor evaluated by his method. The Department of Mineralogy
undertook the shipping of his specimens back to Ann Arbor, to await laboratory analysis on his return. Since pegmatites develop from highly fluid magma,
they represent a formation halfway between those masses slowly cooled from
molten rock and those minerals deposited in veins by superheated waters;
hence, a study of pegmatites can help to fill out our knowledge of the earth.
Dr. Heinrich is in the process of making this study.

Mathematics

Only one grant, to Dr. Frank Harary, has been made from the Rackham
funds for research in mathematics. On May 21, 1953, he received $1,600 to
continue his applications of mathematical graphs to social psychology and
statistical mechanics, thereby strengthening the mathematical basis of the
work of the University's Research Center for Group Dynamics, and, with the
collaboration of Dr. George E. Uhlenbeck, Professor of Physics, making statistical mechanics more useful.

Geology

Geologists have received a total of $25,083.11. Eight men and one institute
have engaged in fifteen projects; explorations have ranged from Hudson Bay
to Mexico. For the year 1942–43, Professor Kenneth K. Landes received $500
to map water tables and test electrically the flow and porosity in subterranean
rock. Inserting two suitably spaced electrodes in the earth, he mapped changes
in resistance as he changed their location. From this research came his paper
entitled *Ground-Water Exploration by Earth Resistivity Methods*.[28]

Three geologists made paleontological explorations. For the year 1936–37,
Professor Lewis B. Kellum, Director of the Museum of Paleontology, received
$1,000 to begin what developed into three related projects dealing with Mexi-
can fossilized fauna. The Geological Society of America gave another $1,000
to make up the salary of Dr. R. W. Imlay, Professor Kellum's assistant. This
project led to a grant of $150, in 1941–42, for the compilation of a geologic
map of the southern half of Mexico, and to a grant of $1,222.86, in the same
year, for studies on the Coahuila Massif in northern Mexico. Several publications resulted.

Professor Claude W. Hibbard, Curator of Vertebrate Paleontology in the Museum, received two grants in 1951 and 1952, amounting to $5,016, to assist in the continuation of his extensive research on Pleistocene and Cenozoic vertebrate microfossils. For fifteen years Professor Hibbard had been examining successive layers of fauna in the high plains of the western United States. He had located, in Meade County, Kansas, the only known successive deposits of Pleistocene vertebrates in North America. In this semiarid region, he had discovered the remains of a new Pleistocene species of rice rat, at altitudes above 2,500 feet. With his Rackham grants he continued to collect and study specimens of this and other small vertebrates. Since descendants of this rat live today only in humid climates, at altitudes not exceeding 800 feet, Professor Hibbard opened an entirely new page of Pleistocene history. His report throws considerable light on research in the field:

> Collecting vertebrate fossils is a great gamble since one is never sure of results. Last year (1951) was the poorest year due to excessive rain that I have ever encountered in a semiarid region in 24 years of field experience. We worked from sun-up to sunset all summer and finally recovered from a bed of a small stream (which should have been dry) 12 species of mammals which brings the total of fauna to 15 mammals, 1 turtle, a few birds, a frog or two and two toads, besides a large invertebrate fauna. We removed, dried and washed over one ton of matrix for each specimen (mammal jaw) recovered.

Another significant fossil was uncovered with the aid of Rackham money. In 1936, a relative of Michigan's Professor Ermine C. Case, employed on the Fort Peck federal dam near Glasgow, Montana, discovered some prehistoric remains. In the summer of 1938, Professor Case and his workers, assisted by a $2,000 grant, chiseled the fossilized bones from their rock bed. Uncovered, the skeleton proved to be that of a forty-foot-long duck-billed dinosaur, on its side, with neck and head thrown forward, looking very much like a horse, dead on the battlefield. A missing portion of the tail and part of one hind leg were replaced from other bones scattered in the area. Crated and shipped to Ann Arbor, the 8,000 pound skeleton was assembled where it is on exhibit today in the University Museums. It is the only complete dinosaur fossil in the Museums. Beside it is a rare imprint in rock of the texture of the animal's skin.

Aside from a survey of the Tertiary geological history of the basins north of Salt Lake in Utah, made in 1945 by Professor Armand J. Eardley with the assistance of a $150 grant, all of the remaining investigations were centered around the Great Lakes. The Great Lakes Research Institute, for example, which was organized as an activity of the Graduate School and established by the Regents on May 25, 1945, for "the encouragement and integration of studies of the physical, chemical, biological and other aspects of the Great Lakes and related areas," received a $3,500 grant, in 1947, for a geological coring of the bottom of Lake Erie. Working from a raft, jerry-built from telephone poles and oil drums and towed by their boat, an expedition under the direction of Professor J. T. Wilson in the summer of 1948 obtained twenty-one corings to discover the "nature, amount, and horizontal and vertical variation in the bottom sediment," and "to establish a post-glacial chronology based on the varved sediment expected in the lake basin." The United States Geological Survey assisted with salaries and expenses. In 1949, the Horace H. Rackham Fund gave $4,000 more to continue the project, specifically for building a raft sturdy enough for work farther offshore. The Institute is now seeking additional funds to complete its survey.

Another Great Lakes project is incomplete. In 1942, Professor Irving D. Scott, an eminent geologist and an authority on the sand dunes of Michigan, received $5,200 from a friend to relieve him from teaching to complete his life-long study of the Michigan dunes, which are of special interest because they do not migrate, as do the dunes of the desert, but either grow from tufts of grass into tree-bearing hills, or cave into the surf to grow again. The Horace H. Rackham Fund granted $2,000 more for aerial photographs and cartographical assistance. The study was interrupted by the war. Professor Scott retired in 1947, and the final analysis and charting of the dunes remains unfinished.

Two other geologists have conducted five productive investigations. In 1943, Professor Kenneth K. Landes accepted a contract with the Michigan Department of Conservation, Geological Survey Division, to study exposed limestones and shales in the vicinity of Mackinac Straits, and to trace the formations underground to oil-bearing regions to the south. Aside from mapping limestone, oil, gas, and water, Professor Landes was particularly interested in testing his theory as to the origin of the brecciated extrusions around Mackinac—the arches, castles, and grotesque shapes which had puzzled observers since the time of Father Marquette. From the Horace H. Rackham Fund, he received additional support, amounting to $896.19. He was assisted by Professor George M. Ehlers, Curator of Paleozoic Invertebrates in the University's Museum of Paleontology. The resulting book includes a chapter on the glacial geology of the region, by Professor George M. Stanley.[29]

Professor Landes clarified the order of the successive depositions of stone. He found that the monoliths of breccia had not been heaped together atop dolomite and limestone at the ancient salt-sea bottom, but that they had been formed by fragments which dropped from the underside of the hard-rock strata, as subterranean water ate away the layer of salt beneath. Later, as the earth's crust heaved upward, these piles of rubble, internally cemented by calcifying waters and surrounded by newer and softer rock, were pushed above the water and exposed to the weather. Professor Landes made a subsequent study of the geology of southeastern Michigan and adjoining areas with another grant of $1,535 (1946–47) from the Rackham endowment.

In May, 1939, Professor Stanley received $700 to make the first of three analyses of ancient shorelines connected with the Great Lakes basin. Since the Great Lakes lie on the southwestern slope of "what might be called a great dome of postglacial deformation (a movement, according to Great Lakes gauges . . . still in progress),"[30] Professor Stanley traveled to Hudson Bay, situated near the apex of the dome, to examine waterlines left in previous ages. His proposal stated that "nothing accurate is known of the central part or northerly slope of this dome, and pertinent data have been desired by many geologists." An assistant to operate the spirit level, and Eskimo guides and helpers accompanied him in schooner and freight canoes owned by the Hudson Bay Company, and he completed his measurements. His findings, as well as the findings of his two subsequent projects, were published in the *Bulletin of the Geological Society of America*. The first of these two projects was a study of the late postglacial beaches near Killarney, Ontario ($240, 1940–41), undertaken partly to assist the Museum of Anthropology in dating specimens found there; the second was a study of varve and peat deposits to determine the antiquity of glacial Lake Algonquin ($754.26, 1945–46).

Engineering

In 1945, a grant of $5,500 was made to the Department of Chemical and Metallurgical Engineering for the purchase of a new type of X-ray diffraction unit, the Geiger-counter X-ray spectrometer. This instrument is a powerful tool for the study of crystal structure, of the surface conditions of solids, and of colloidal particles. It is important for research in engineering and in other fields, such as physical chemistry and mineralogy.

Another important tool for research in a number of branches of the physical sciences, the electron microscope, was purchased by a Rackham research grant to the Physics Department, but it, again, was also intended for use by others. Professor Lars Thomassen, of the Department of Chemical and Metallurgical Engineering, used it to study the structure of protective coatings on aluminum alloys ($3,003.20, 1942–46); Professor Alfred H. White,[31] then Chairman of the Department, used it in his studies of protective coatings on magnesium alloys and of the carbonaceous products of heated organic matter ($2,885.75, 1942–45); Professor Donald L. Katz,[32] who succeeded Professor White as Department Chairman, used it to study the structure of oils and industrial solids ($4,200, 1942–46).

An earlier grant to Professor Katz ($800, 1940) resulted in his three-hundred page *Bibliography of Physical Behavior of Hydrocarbons Under Pressure and Related Phenomena*.[33] An earlier grant had also been made to Professor White ($500, 1940–41) and helped to culminate the work of more than thirty years. In 1911 Professor White had published his discovery that structures of Portland cement changed volume when immersed in water, or, after having been immersed, when exposed to air, even after long periods in either element.

Then followed years of chemical analyses of industrial cements and successive measurements of their concrete products, yielding, by the time of Professor White's Rackham grant in 1940, ten research papers and a unique collection of concrete bars with histories reaching back for more than thirty years. In 1930, Professor White had considered his observations closed, but a casual inspection of his bars in 1940 showed some unexpected disintegration, and he used the $500 grant in his work of assessing the changes that had occurred over the decade, and particularly, of measuring the effect of magnesium in concrete, evident only after long periods of time. He presented his findings in a paper before the American Society for Testing Materials.

Other Rackham grants have covered a wide range of projects in engineering, including the following studies: the effects of atomic blasts on steel structures, by Professor Bruce Johnston ($3,000, 1952–53); nitrogen in steel, by Professor Clair E. Upthegrove ($76.43, 1942–43); the effect of oxygen upon austenite grain size of steel, by Professor Maurice Sinnot ($634.59, 1948–49); the effect of alloying elements on the austenite transformation in cast iron, by Professor William P. Wood ($500, 1940–41); electronic flow at ultra-high frequencies, by Professor William G. Dow ($743.72, 1941–43); liquid flow through industrial filters, by Professor Lloyd E. Brownell ($1,400, 1949–50); the percolation of water in deep soil as an aid in draining highways and airports, by Professor William S. Housel ($1,751.25, 1939–47); the combustion of oil-burning engines, by Professor Edward T. Vincent ($558.26, 1940–43); the disposal of city garbage with city sewage, by Professor William C. Hoad ($317.65, 1940–41); variation in muscular movement patterns with changes of speed, by Professor Charles B. Gordy ($111.62, 1945–46); the stresses borne by structural columns, by Professor Jan A. Van den Broek ($1,223.04, 1938–43); the structural action of various types of rigid joints, by Professor Lawrence C. Maugh ($950.43, 1939–40).

Altogether, engineering has received a total of $28,155.94 from the Horace H. Rackham Fund.

Astronomy

The investment of Rackham money in the University's astronomical observatories has extended over a long period of time and has resulted in the construction and purchase of important, elaborate equipment. For work at the Lamont-Hussey Observatory in South Africa, the Rackham Trustees gave $6,000 (1934), and, over the years, the Horace H. Rackham Fund added $25,054.85. To the McMath-Hulbert Observatory, at Lake Angelus, the Trustees gave $25,000, and the Horace H. Rackham Fund, $10,900. Two other astronomy projects have, together, received $1,250 in grants. The total from the Horace H. Rackham Fund has amounted to $37,204.85.

On October 28, 1926, Professor William J. Hussey, who for years had planned a study of double stars from a southern station, died in London while on his way to establish a University observatory at Bloemfontein, South Africa, for which funds had been given by the Honorable Robert P. Lamont, of Detroit, then Secretary of Commerce of the United States. Dr. Richard A. Rossiter, Professor Hussey's assistant, took over the assignment, which lasted until his retirement on December 31, 1952. "The building with ample office, library, and other space was completed in February, 1928. The 56-foot dome and 27-inch Lamont Refractor were then erected and completed for the beginning of a regular observing program on May 9, 1928,"[34] and Professor Rossiter began his twenty-five-year-long study of the southern skies, alone except for one or two assistants in the first five years, and an increasing number of visiting astronomers.

When Mr. Lamont's support ceased in 1934, the Rackham Trustees gave Professor Rossiter $6,000 for another year. At the end of the year 1935–36, private funds were found to carry the project until July 1937; then for five more years, on the single condition that Professor Rossiter remain to continue his work, the Union of South Africa provided four-fifths of the expenses, and Bloemfontein, one-fifth. When the five-year period expired on April 1, 1942, the Board of Governors of the Graduate School made a $1,000 Rackham grant, which, supplemented by the contingency fund of the University Observatories, and by a balance left from South African gifts, maintained the project for one more year. Finally, beginning in 1944, the Lamont-Hussey Observatory found a place in the regular University budget. For the entire quarter-century of Professor Rossiter's residence, the municipality of Bloemfontein furnished him a rent-free house. At the end of last year Professor Rossiter retired, and the University's stay in South Africa ended with its twenty-fifth year. The Observatory was leased for use during the current year, and then, unless other tenants appear, it will be abandoned and the optical parts shipped back to Ann Arbor.

The first years of the project were devoted chiefly to locating and charting double stars. Mr. M. K. Jessup discovered 803, and Mr. H. F. Donner, 1,030. Professor Rossiter's own list eventually came to well over 7,000, making him the most successful double-star observer since Sir John Herschel. Lists were published periodically in the *Memoirs of the Royal Astronomical Society,* and the final results are expected to be published by the University as a memorial volume to Professor Hussey, who brought the project into existence.

The later years of the project resulted in a careful remeasurement of the stars already discovered, an occasional discovery of a new pair, and the charting of a wide segment of the southern sky in new detail. The station was exceptionally well situated for the purpose, commanding, as it does, the area of the southern sky richest in double stars. Frequency varies from a few pairs in some sectors, to over 500 pairs in the seventh hour. Over 13,000 people used the telescope on regular visitors' nights.

From 1948 through 1951, another Rackham project, with grants totaling $24,054.85, was carried out at Bloemfontein in conjunction with the Mt. Wilson Observatory. Using a telescope loaned by Mt. Wilson, the University conducted a three-fold study of the southern skies that proposed, as stated in Professor Leo Goldberg's outline: (1) to look for certain "comparatively rare stars and nebulae . . .," especially for three types of cool red stars. "Many of the objects of this search are infrequently encountered and poorly understood. Individually, they are the rare birds that upset our ideas on the structure of the stars and nebulae and collectively their distribution is of great significance in the study of galactic structure"; (2) to keep under surveillance the Magellanic Clouds, the two nearest of the extragalactic nebulae, lying in the Milky Way near the Southern Cross. These "contain large numbers of variable stars," and the "spectroscopic changes associated with the light variations should yield results of great importance"; (3) to make spectral classifications of the Lamont-Hussey double stars.

The astronomer chosen for this work was Mr. Karl G. Henize, who had recently taken his master's degree at the University of Virginia, working there with a telescope similar to the one loaned by Mt. Wilson, "a small, but extremely powerful and effective . . . 10½-inch telescope, accommodating 14-inch-square photographic plates, with a wide field of view and a special red-corrected lens which makes possible the easy detection of nebulae and peculiar stars." Mr. Henize proved to have the mental and physical stamina which Professor Goldberg had sought among a number of applicants for the job. After visits to Mt. Wilson and Ann Arbor, Mr. Henize sailed from Trinidad on November 26, 1948, arriving in Bloemfontein on December 17. By the time the telescope arrived, March 14, 1949, local contractors with designs, direction, and help from Professor Rossiter and Mr. Henize, had completed a small, new building near the Lamont-Hussey Observatory. By March 30, 1949, Mr. Henize had assembled and installed the telescope.

Professor Goldberg and Professor Freeman D. Miller planned and directed the project. In exchange for an option on 2,200 square degrees of the heavens, Mt. Wilson furnished the telescope and left 8,000 square degrees free for the University, which provided the location and the photographic plates. Preliminary conclusions from the Magellanic-Cloud observations were presented in Ann Arbor on June 23, 1950, at a symposium on "The Structure of the Galaxy," held at the dedication of the University's Portage Lake Observatory.[35] The project produced an abundance of publications and photographs for both the University and Mt. Wilson. Mr. Henize, by agreement, returned to the University to complete his doctor's degree, using a part of the data.

Under two Rackham grants, totaling $800 (1939 and 1941), another project, a study of peculiar and variable stellar spectra, was undertaken in Ann Arbor and at the Harvard University Observatory by Professor Dean B. McLaughlin, who, with Mr. Henize,[36] completed his report in 1950.

The account of the University's McMath Hulbert Observatory, at Lake Angelus, like that of the Lamont-Hussey Laboratory in South Africa, must be carried back some years to place the Rackham contributions in perspective. On December 15, 1931, Mr. Francis C. McMath, a builder of bridges, Mr. Robert R. McMath, his son, also a bridge builder and manufacturer, and Judge Henry S. Hulbert, a Detroit jurist, gave to the University the astronomical observatory which they had built on Mr. Robert McMath's property at Lake Angelus, near Pontiac, Michigan. These three men, whose long-continued interest in and knowledge of the subject placed them high on the list of the country's amateur astronomers, had previously (June 14, 1929) been made Honorary Curators of Astronomical Observatories by the University, as a consequence of their earlier gifts and help in constructing the Angell Hall Observatory. At Lake Angelus they had developed "new and unique mechanical methods of making cinegraphic records of the moon, planets, and other stellar objects."[37] Originally the plan had been to make educational movies, but the films immediately revealed immense scientific potentialities.

In 1935 and 1936 the Trustees of the Rackham estate gave the University $25,000[38] for a new solar tower adjacent to the Observatory. At the same time, the McGregor Fund of Washington, D.C., gave $7,000, the beginning of substantial yearly support that continued for a number of years. Many private individuals, including the three astronomers themselves, added sizable gifts of money.

The new tower was completed in 1936, designed entirely by Mr. Robert McMath after he had studied installations at Mt. Wilson and Pasadena. Modifications in optical train suggested by Dr. Edison Pettit and a system of electrical rate controls invented by Mr. McMath made the tower, "though inferior in height to the California towers, . . . one of the most powerful in use at the present time."[39] The Lake Angelus Observatory made the first continuous record of the changes of the moon, which disclosed accurately, in varying lengths of shadow, the heights of mountains and the depths of craters, and which, for "the density of gases and rates of expansion in the solar chromosphere, opened a rich field of research hitherto untouched."[40] President Ruthven persuaded Mr. McMath to resign the presidency of the Motors Metal Manufacturing Company to become, on February 1, 1939, full-time Director of the Observatory and Professor of Astronomy, posts which he still holds. From 1936 through 1939, the Board of Governors of the Graduate School furnished $5,900 in Rackham money for a research assistant at Lake Angelus.

A Rackham research grant of $550, in 1945, was made to Assistant Professor Robley C. Williams for the determination of the distribution of energy in infra-red stellar spectra, and resulted, in 1946,[41] in the *Spectrophotometric Atlas of Stellar Spectra* (with Mr. W. A. Hiltner) and a number of related papers.

Chemistry

In chemistry, eleven men have conducted projects under grants amounting to $75,833.71. As with the majority of the projects in the physical sciences, most of the money went for the salaries of technical assistants. Because of the demand for chemists in industrial and governmental laboratories, it has often been difficult to find competent graduate students for research assistantships. In several instances this situation has been met by bringing in foreign scholars, who welcome an opportunity for work in this country at the conservative salaries possible. Such is the case with Dr. Otto Vogl, who this year has come from an Austrian university to assist Professor Christian S. Rondestvedt in studying the chemistry of decomposition ($4,000, 1953–54).

One of the first such foreign scientists to come to Michigan was Dr. Ying Fu, Chairman of the Department of Chemistry at the University of Chungking, a Michigan Ph.D. and former student of Professor Floyd E. Bartell, on whose project ($7,659.85, 1936–47) he came to work. Driven from university to university by war, Dr. Fu wrote Professor Bartell (April 6, 1944) to inquire about possibilities of work at Michigan: ". . . . financially and intellectually, the Chinese universities are on a diet, a maintenance diet way below par at that. As I grow older and wiser (?), I become more philosophical and fatalistic, otherwise my hair would have become gray long ago."

For some years previous to the arrival of Dr. Fu, Professor Bartell had been studying the surface properties of solids. In 1938–39, a Rackham grant had provided the assistance of Dr. G. L. Mack of the New York Agricultural Experiment Station, who had published widely in the field, and Professor Bartell had undertaken a study of the surface properties of solid and liquid gallium, a practical purpose of which was to determine "the adhesive forces at the metal-oil interface" in the bearings of machinery. With Dr. Fu, Professor Bartell continued his investigations to find a reliable method of determining the surface tension of solids, to measure the tendency of particles to aggregate and to disperse. He set down the importance of his work in his request for funds (June, 1938):

Nearly all natural processes involve free surface energy changes. Practically every physiological reaction is dependent upon such changes. This includes every step of life processes and growth, functions of the different organs, and various diseases of the organs . . . . What are the causes of the great but rapid changes which occur in the permeability of the protoplasmic materials?

With Dr. Ying Fu, Professor Bartell worked out and published an impressive number of specific answers to the general question.

Earlier, the University had gained another noted chemist, Professor Kasimir Fajans of Munich, Germany, who, as a result of the prewar tensions there, accepted an appointment here in the fall of 1936. Assisted by various Rackham grants from 1941 through 1953, amounting, in all, to $17,149.86,

Professor Fajans studied the dispersion of light when molecules, solutions, and crystals form from free atoms and ions. Two of his assistants, Mr. Juan Curet and Mr. Theodore Berlin, were Rackham Predoctoral Fellows. With Mr. Berlin, Professor Fajans examined the electronic structure of chemical systems, closely connected with his study of dispersion. Under his direction, Miss Jean Chien-Han Chu obtained "results concerning the structure of concentrated solutions of lithium perchlorate in ether and acetone." In 1944, Professor Fajans wrote the Graduate School of his work:

The theoretical research outlined in the application of February, 1943, has been developed since that time in several directions in collaboration with Mr. Theodore Berlin on the chemical-physical aspect, with Mr. Peter Smith on the chemical aspect, with Dr. Wilfred Kaplan in Ann Arbor and Dr. Max Pernt in New York on the mathematical aspect and with Professor L. S. Ramsdell on the crystalographical aspect. The results obtained give a very good support for the new approach to the electronic structure of molecules and crystals.

With a grant of $2,869 for the year 1949–50, Professor Peter A. S. Smith, mentioned above, was assisted in his research into the chemistry of synthesis. Earlier, under his direction, Mr. Bernard Brown had made a discovery which "led to the synthesis of a number of new compounds . . . and to greatly improved synthesis for several previously known substances, all of which are potentially important intermediates in the synthesis of drugs and certain alkaloids." Professor Smith's Rackham research into the synthesis of nitrogen heterocycles by means of aryl azides was assisted by Mr. Joseph H. Boyer. The project worked out practical methods for the druggist, and increased the general knowledge of the nature of synthesis.

Helped by grants totaling $15,700 (1939–49), Professor Werner E. Bachmann carried on his distinguished research on the synthesis of sex hormones and antimalarials. This work led to numerous publications and contributed to his fame as an organic chemist. In recognition of the position he had attained in this field he was elected to the National Academy of Sciences.

Other studies in the synthesis of drugs were carried on by Professor Frederick F. Blicke, of the Department of Pharmaceutical Chemistry. With grants totaling $4,200 (1939–43) he worked on the production of substitutes for ergot and other antispasmodic drugs.

In 1936–37, Professors Alfred L. Ferguson and Lee O. Case, with a Rackham grant of $2,655, directed a partly successful attempt to redetermine, by experiment, the standards of measurement for electrolytic conductivity. In 1949 and 1950, two grants, totaling $4,900, were made to Professor Ferguson to compile a bibliography, local and foreign, and to make a thorough critical study of the literature of electrochemical polarization and overvoltage, later published.

Under the supervision, first of Professor C. S. Schoepfle, but later under the direction of his colleague Professor Lawrence O. Brockway, $13,400 from the Horace H. Rackham Fund was granted, between 1938 and 1944, toward the purchase of chemical research equipment. For example, of the $4,500 needed for an electron diffraction outfit essential to Professor Brockway's research, the Chemistry Department provided $2,300, the Midgley Foundation of the Ohio State University added $1,000, and the Horace H. Rackham Fund gave $1,200. The request for assistance in buying the equipment (February 8, 1938) states that at the Massachusetts Institute of Technology Dr. Brockway, with Professor Linus Pauling, was

> ... largely responsible for the development of the electron diffraction method, first used by Mark and Wierl, for the determination of the structure of molecules. The procedure consists in causing a beam of electrons traveling with a uniform velocity to intersect a jet of gas, the scattered electrons being recorded on a photographic film set at right angles to the direction of the initial beam. From the diffraction pattern obtained, which differs for each compound, it is possible to determine the exact arrangement of the atoms in the molecule, as well as the distance between atoms. The electron diffraction method is one of the most modern and useful tools for the determination of molecular structure, and opens up a wide and important field of investigation.

At that time Professor Brockway had been co-author, with Professor Pauling, of nine papers, and sole author or senior author of nineteen more; he has continued to publish widely.

In 1941, Professor Brockway received another grant of $2,500 to construct a mass spectrograph, and in 1944, $7,500 to buy one of the ten cameras manufactured by the General Electric Company, under high priorities, for photographing the diffraction of solid surfaces. In addition to its investigational importance, this camera is extremely useful in the study of machined surfaces and the effect on them of corrosion, wear, lubrication, and catalytic activity. Under still a fourth grant, Professor Brockway, in the year 1943–44, analyzed the structure of "new organic fluorides for possible war uses." The Horace H. Rackham Fund and the Naval Research Laboratory each paid half of the $2,500 salary of Mr. Robert Livingston, Professor Brockway's assistant on the project.

During the year 1951–52, Professor Wyman R. Vaughan received a grant of $3,000 for an assistant, plus $300 for supplies, to make "an initial investigation of an experimental character into an area of stereochemistry about which relatively little is known": the replacement of functional groups by hydrogen.

Physics

The first request from the Physics Department for a grant from Rackham funds was made to the Trustees of the Horace H. Rackham and Mary A. Rackham Fund by Professor Harrison M. Randall, then Chairman of the Department, who asked for $25,000 for nuclear research and the building of a cyclotron. The Trustees granted his request on June 14, 1935, and the cyclotron was built and installed in the basement of the Physics Building (later to become the Harrison M. Randall Laboratory of Physics), where it is now. Its operation is under the supervision of Associate Professor William C. Parkinson.

It resembles a huge, squat spool on end. The thick spool ends, which look something like bellows, are actually coils of copper ribbon painted orange. They carry the electric current to magnetize the cyclotron's steel magnet, which is the framework holding the spool ends. Into the central drum and out the other side extend the ducts along which deuterons are fired at the target-matter, and out of which neutrons, Gamma rays, and other high-energy radiations are filtered, directed, and controlled. The stationary central drum and the magnetic field give the particles an energizing whirl which finally sends them, like cream from a separator, off at a tangent. These rays are then carried by means of a duct through a four-foot wall of water in metal tanks, and by this means workers are protected from stray radiation. In eighteen years, no one has received the slightest damage from the use of the cyclotron.

For those eighteen years it has been a powerful research tool for the study of nuclear structure, for the production of radioactive isotopes to be used in chemical research and in medical research and treatment, and for the training of badly needed nuclear scientists. It has just been rebuilt with money allocated by the Atomic Energy Commission and by the Michigan Memorial–Phoenix Project and now operates with a precision, selectivity, and beam-intensity surpassed by none. In the atomic age of today, it is more useful than ever before—a statement that is, itself, a tribute to the far-sighted vision of those who planned and financed it, the second and, when built, the largest cyclotron in the world.

Aside from his wise administration of his Department, perhaps Professor Randall's greatest single service to the University was his securing money for, and his assistance and supervision of the construction of this important instrument for research. The following account of its early history is taken from a report by Professor James M. Cork, who was responsible for its design, construction, and early operation:

With the successful operation of the thirty-seven inch cyclotron at Berkeley in 1934, giving deuterons with an energy of 3.5 million electron volts, the importance of this machine became apparent. The design of a larger instrument was begun by the writer in 1935, then on leave as a Research Associate at the University of California. This larger (50 inch) cyclotron was initiated in 1936 and at once yielded more energetic particles than any other existing device. Two years later it was surpassed in output by a new 60-inch Berkeley instrument.

The Michigan Cyclotron was built when prices were at an all-time low, with copper at six cents per pound and steel at twenty-one dollars per ton. The Detroit Edison Company very generously furnished much of the accompanying electric equipment. As a result the total cost of the instrument was under twenty-five thousand which is less than one-tenth of its present replacement value.

For the first ten years this instrument was constantly in operation and yielded phenomenally rich results. Not only in physics but in the allied sciences of chemistry, biology, metallurgy, engineering, mineralogy, and medicine were the products of the cyclotron successfully employed. About fifteen Ph.D. thesis investigations in various fields made use of these radioactive materials.

Of the great number of currently known radioactive isotopes perhaps one-fourth were observed and recognized in this laboratory for the first time .... For a nine-month period in

1943 the cyclotron was operated under contract with the Metallurgical Project of the University of Chicago, Manhattan District. During this period the instrument operated on a continuous twenty-four hour basis in the study of the failure of metals exposed to radiation in order to select the most stable element for use in piles or reactors then under construction. Aluminum appeared to be the most satisfactory metal in this respect.

In addition to the $100,200 granted in the first four years for work with the cyclotron, grants in more recent years have brought the total for research with the cyclotron, to date, to $141,514.06. This figure does not include the original $25,000 from the Rackham Trustees. Research with the cyclotron has received support, also, from the Atomic Energy Commission and from the Michigan Memorial–Phoenix Project.

The request for a grant to purchase and operate an electron microscope came, likewise, from Professor Randall, with endorsements from scientists of other departments who saw a use for it in their work. With Rackham grants totaling $15,516.15, in 1940 and 1941, it was bought and put into operation in the Physics Building, under the direction of Professor O. S. Duffendack. Rackham research grants, through 1953, for research involving the microscope have totaled $28,806.34.

In February, 1944, Professor Duffendack was joined in his study of metallic vapors[42] by Professor H. R. Crane and in 1946 by Assistant Professor Robley C. Williams of the Astronomy Department. In August, 1946, the University promoted Dr. Williams from Assistant Professor of Astronomy to Associate Professor of Physics, his basic field. At the same time he received a grant from the American Cancer Society of New York to begin the examination of protein macromolecules with the electron microscope, which was to lead him, with Professor Crane and Dr. Ralph W. G. Wyckoff, an expert in virus diseases, to work out the techniques which today largely make the instrument effective in this work. Turning from the stars to look down the microscope into another universe, Professor Williams devised a method of casting shadows upon infinitesimal contours of matter, throwing them into a relief not unlike that of the shadowed craters of the moon.

Rackham research projects involving the use of the electron microscope and contributing to its upkeep have been carried on by members of the faculties of the College of Engineering, the Department of Bacteriology, and others, and many research projects not supported directly by Rackham grants have been indirectly assisted by the use of the microscope. It is now under the direction of Assistant Professor Cyrus Levinthal and is available to all interested departments.

The instrument looks very much like an ordinary microscope, some eight feet tall, standing straight up from the floor. Its direct magnification of about 14,000 diameters can be extended up to about 40,000—greater extensions are of little use—by enlarging its photographic plates. Professor Williams was chiefly responsible for the technique of interpreting the photographic data, as

Horace H. Rackham Educational Memorial

well as for the shadowing process developed with Professors Duffendack and Crane and Dr. Wyckoff in the studies of metal mists on collodion. Instead of examining the metal itself, they used the metal and its flat collodion support as a means for examining other things. The process may be likened to drifting a metal fog slantwise across tiny hills and valleys of colorless fingernail polish. When the metal hardens, the terrain can be revealed from above by electronic light. For inspecting the solid surfaces of metals, a collodion replica is made and the metallic fog drifted on. Similar collodion castings are made of viruses, or the virus itself may be subjected to the metallic shadowing.

Seven other projects have been assisted by $11,646.10 in Rackham grants.

Professor Charles F. Meyer received a grant of $395.75 (1938–39) to assist in the construction of a modification of the Twyman-Green interferometer, for the examination of the degree of perfection of glass prisms and lenses. With a grant of $750 (1938–39), Professor Neil H. Williams was assisted in his research on the production of very short electric waves; this work was an important step in the feat of bridging the gap between the short electric waves and the long-wavelength infrared radiation with which Professor Randall had worked. In 1938–39, Professor Ralph A. Sawyer, with Dr. Raymond R. Waggoner, of the Department of Psychiatry, developed a spectrographic technique for diagnosing lead poisoning, a sometimes obscure and misinterpreted disease, by detecting the presence of minute amounts of lead in the body tissues and fluids.

A study of mesons and other fundamental physical particles by new techniques was begun by Professor William A. Nierenberg in the fall of 1949, with a $2,500 grant. It was taken over in December, 1950, by Professor William C. Parkinson and is still under way. The Physics Department furnished shop services and parts to build the necessary equipment, and the Rackham grant was expended for a research assistant and for travel to Columbia University and the Massachusetts Institute of Technology for consultation.

With $1,500, in 1951 Dr. Donald A. Glaser built a chamber holding superheated liquid at high pressure, and this device permitted him to observe bubbles in the ionized path of a cosmic-ray particle when pressure was released. By this means Dr. Glaser was able to verify a theory he had previously developed as to the workings of radiation on liquids, and to point the way by which a new type of radiation detector might be developed. Some of his findings have been published.[43]

In 1948 Professor Wayne E. Hazen received $2,500 to assist him in his extensive research that has recently won him a Guggenheim Fellowship and brought him recognition as one of the leading authorities on cosmic rays. Taking cloud chambers, made for the purpose, to the mountains near Denver, Colorado, he studied the interaction of cosmic rays and nuclei at high altitudes.[44] The following year he turned his attention in the opposite direction, making observations in the deep salt mines, in Detroit, which resulted in his studies: "Cloud Chamber Study of Cosmic Rays Underground,"[45] "The Absorption of Penetrating Cosmic Rays Underground,"[46] and "The Ratio of Electrons to Mesons 1100 Feet Underground."[47]

At the time of this writing, Professor Harrison M. Randall is still doing active and productive research, thirteen years after his retirement at the end of the semester following his seventieth birthday, December 17, 1940. Already well known for his work on the infrared spectra of molecules, he began, in 1949, with a Rackham research grant of $3,000.35, to study the application of infrared spectroscopy to biological materials. His work has since been supported by funds from governmental and other sources. He has published widely in this field. Using the intricate and painstaking techniques that he has developed, he and his assistants are now determining the minute variation in differing strains of tuberculosis bacilli.

Altogether, grants in physics from the Horace H. Rackham Fund have totaled $197,277.73.

Biological Sciences

Over the years, the biological sciences have received $311,277.73 in Rackham research grants. Research in botany, zoology, and biology is covered by this heading, with biology including a number of studies by medical scientists, chemists, psychologists, one anthropologist, and others.

Botany

Ten botanists have received a total of $40,515.71 for sixteen projects, carried on in Ann Arbor and in places as far removed as Alaska, Puerto Rico, Guatemala, and the South Seas. Aided by grants amounting to $3,846.40 (1951–54), Professor Stanley A. Cain has been preparing a *Pollen Atlas* of northeastern America. Professor Dow V. Baxter of the School of Natural Resources ($3,500, 1951–53) carried on a series of studies of the fungi which destroy Alaskan and Canadian timbers. Professor Harley H. Bartlett, Director of the Botanical Gardens, was assisted in an extended study of the botany and of the Indonesian languages of the Philippines, by a $1,000 Rackham Research grant, 1947.

Two books have been completed with the aid of Rackham research grants. Covering an area which, as he stated in his request, had "never heretofore been comprehensively dealt with by anyone with considerable first-hand knowledge of the organisms involved," Professor Frederick K. Sparrow culminated a ten-year study of water fungi, which he had carried on at various universities— Harvard, Cornell, Cambridge, and Copenhagen—and at the Woods Hole

Oceanographic Institute, with his *Aquatic Phycomycetes, Exclusive of the Sapolegniaceae and Pythium* ($498.94, 1938–39).[48] Professor William Randalph Taylor, botanist for Operation Crossroads, the atomic bomb tests conducted in 1946, was enabled, by a $1,199.78 Rackham grant (1948–49), to complete his *Plants of Bikini and Other Northern Marshall Islands*, another step in "his extensive pioneer study of the marine algae of the Pacific."[49]

Three botanists have made explorations with partial support from Rackham research funds. In 1938–39 Professor Cyrus L. Lundell, with a $1,000 grant, was able to send an assistant to Yucatan to continue his already copious work on a botanical survey of the Maya area that had previously been supported by the University of Michigan and the Carnegie Institute. In the same year, assisted by a $300 grant, Professor Elzada U. Clover, Associate Curator in the Botanical Gardens, joined a group of scientists in several fields on a boat trip down Utah's Green River to the Colorado and on through the Grand Canyon to Boulder Dam. Much of the region had never been investigated scientifically. The expedition was under the leadership of geologist and archeologist Norman Nevills, who designed the boats after having previously navigated the Colorado. Professor Clover, who served as photographer and botanist, published a number of studies after the trip, particularly on the cacti of the region. In 1946 she was invited to join a scientific cruise by schooner through the South Seas and around the world, and received a $1,600 Rackham grant for that purpose, but a tidal wave wrecked the ship in Honolulu before the expedition started, and Professor Clover redirected her travels through Texas, Mexico, and Guatemala, collecting and tracing the migrations of cacti. Professor William C. Steere was appointed to an exchange professorship at the University of Puerto Rico in 1938–39 and received a $600 Rackham grant to enable him to extend his study of mosses. For further studies in this field, Professor Steere received three other grants, totaling $3,348.32 (1938–48).

Two men have earned distinction with studies of the reproduction and growth of plants. Professor Felix G. Gustafson has induced the development of fruits without fertilization, studied hormones and vitamins, and traced, with radioactive phosphorus manufactured by the University's cyclotron, the paths of minerals up plant stems. For two projects, with many ramifications, he received $9,222.27 between 1937 and 1953. Under grants for two projects totaling $14,400 (1939–40), Professor Carl D. LaRue also made explorations into the reproductive secrets of plants, studies which have become identified with his name. For the first time in botanical history he succeeded in growing, in test tubes, buds and roots from generating tissue taken from the seeds and pollen of plants, and in transplanting the live tissue from one culture to another. This work, as well as that of Professor Gustafson, is basic, leading to a better understanding of plant growth and of the living organism.

Zoology

Grants in zoology have amounted to $148,285.04 and have supported twenty-six men in thirty-six laboratory and field projects. One project ($4,623.56, 1947–49) was bibliographical: Professor Theodore H. Hubbell, Curator of Insects in the Museum of Zoology, prepared an index-catalogue to the literature on the Orthoptera of the New World. The Orthoptera include such insects as crickets, mantis, and grasshoppers.

Professor Henry van der Schalie, Curator of Mollusks in the Museum of Zoology, has undertaken three Rackham projects ($5,260, 1938–54): the first, a geographic and environmental survey of the land mollusks of Michigan; the second, a pioneer genealogy of fresh-water mussels, traced from their fossilized ancestors; the third, a study of disease-carrying snails, in which he was assisted by Mr. Emile Abdel-Malek, an Egyptian student. In 1953, as Senior Adviser to the Egyptian government for the World Health Organization, Professor van der Schalie was able to extend his study of such snails.

Studies of diseases have also been made in the zoological laboratory. From 1940 to 1950 Professor Arthur E. Woodhead received $4,000 to assist in his detection of the life cycle of the giant kidney worm, which progresses from fish to animals. Other grants, amounting to $26,049.20, have supported studies of nutrition, of genetics, and of growth in tiny organisms; of the development of animal muscles and nerves; of inheritance in frogs; and of the changes in temperature and pressure which make bacteria glow in the sea at night.

With grants from the Horace H. Rackham Fund ($80,093.23, 1940–49)[50] a Heredity Clinic, under the direction of Professor Lee R. Dice, was established and carried on in the Laboratory of Vertebrate Biology until its support was taken over in 1949 by the general funds of the University. By studies of the records and by physical examinations of members of the several hundred families that come each year to the clinic or that are referred to it by physicians, it investigates the role which heredity plays in the production of, or predisposition to, human malformations or diseases. The abnormalities and diseases traced ranged from eye defects, harelip, cleft palate, and clubfoot, to gout,[51] skin diseases, and mental disorders. In some cases, such as gout, hitherto unsuspected or unproved relationships were established. The service rendered, not only to medical science in general but to physicians and to individuals, has been important. In many families, the heredity of particular defects or predispositions can be sufficiently well determined to serve as the basis for advice to the families and to their physicians. Often personal disasters or difficulties can be foreseen and prevented or prepared for. A wide variety of publications has resulted from the Clinic's work, now carried on as one of the activities of the newly formed (1950) Institute of Human Biology, which, with Professor Dice as Director, succeeded the Laboratory of Vertebrate Biology.

Water life has been closely investigated. Professor Frank E. Eggleton, beginning with a grant from the Faculty Research Fund and assisted by a Rackham research grant of $500 in 1940, followed the upswing of life in Geddes Pond when Ann Arbor's new sewage-disposal plant freed the pond from pollution; he also studied Sphaeriidae, small clams of which Michigan has the greatest world population ($600, 1944–45). These are important, from one point of view because they are parasitic hosts and from another point of view because they are food for commercial fish. In 1951–52 ($661.60) Dr. Frank F. Hooper, Biologist in the Institute for Fisheries Research, studied the microscopic mud fauna upon which commercial fish feed. Professor Carl L. Hubbs, with a grant of $1,450, in 1942–43 studied the fishes of the desert, relating species of fish to the geologic history of isolated desert waters. To introduce mosquito fish into Michigan, he was granted $2,099.82 from 1943 to 1945, when the wartime movement of laborers and soldiers threatened to reinfect the local anophele mosquito and to revive the malaria of Michigan's early history.

Under a grant of $1,600 (1945–46) Professor Karl F. Lagler and Professor Hubbs produced their definitive *Fishes of the Great Lakes Region*,[52] and with a grant of $1,275 (1948–49) explored the almost inaccessible lakes, Michigan's highest, of Porcupine Mountains, where the beginnings of life in the path of the receding prehistoric glacier could be traced. Unusual prehistory was also discovered in the fish of the isolated Green River system of Kentucky and Tennessee, by Professor Reeve M. Bailey, Curator of Fishes in the Museum of Zoology, who will be assisted in further work by a $1,900 grant for 1953–54.

The great problem of the origin of species was also attacked by Professor Hubbs, with the aid of a $500 grant in 1937–38. Working with a race of diminutive amazons, an all-female parthenogenetic species, he was able to make analyses of speciation more clear-cut than any ever made on fishes, and to unseat certain common evolutionary assumptions concerning the genesis of systematic traits. During the coming year, Professor Robert Rush Miller, Associate Curator of Fishes, with a grant of $2,500 (1953–54), will study speciation in a viviparous fish of northwestern Mexico.

Working in Mexico in 1952–53, Professor Emmet T. Hooper, Associate Curator of Mammals, studied the environmental distribution of tree squirrels, extending the evolutionary investigations of two earlier projects in southwestern America that had been chiefly concerned with harvest mice. He has received a total of $5,897.63. These studies continued the Museum of Zoology's long-term search for the causes of evolution in isolated mountains and deserts of the Southwest, first conceived and mapped out in 1912, by (then) Professor Alexander G. Ruthven and Mrs. Helen T. Gaige. Paralleling Professor Hooper's work, Dr. W. Frank Blair investigated deermice in the same general region ($425, 1939–40). By trapping, marking, freeing, and recapturing, Dr. Blair measured the distances mice travel from birthplace to mature residence and produced the first concrete evidence of the migratory spans of mammals, generation by generation. Interested also in genetics, he chose the Tularosa Basin of New Mexico because of its marked patches of red soil and of gray soil, which support, respectively, buff and gray variations of the same mouse. (Professor Emmet T. Hooper had previously investigated similar effects of changes of soil and altitude in the Guadalupe Mountains of Texas.)

Professors Pierce Brodkorb, William H. Burt, Norman E. Hartweg, and Laurence C. Stuart increased zoological knowledge and acquired extensive collections for the Museum of Zoology, by expeditions to southern Mexico and Guatemala, its neighbor. On six Rackham-assisted expeditions ($9,350, 1939–40) and a number of others, they ranged, alone or in pairs, from sea level, through deserts and swamps, and on up through rain forest and cloud forest, to an altitude of 14,000 feet. They made extensive collections of birds, amphibians, and reptiles. A new species of lizard, discovered by Professor Stuart, was named by him *Xenosaurus rackhami* in honor of Mr. Rackham.

Biology

Exclusive of botany and zoology, other biological studies have received an aggregate of $122,476.98 in Rackham research grants. Bacteriologists have worked on various microorganisms, from spirochetes to yeasts ($38,010.25); pharmacologists, on drugs and the life processes ($5,689.95); biochemists, on metabolism, amino acids, and antitoxins ($12,657.43); and anatomists and physiologists, on the functions of nerves, glands, blood, and various organs ($40,997.87). Among these investigators were Professors Elizabeth Crosby (anatomy), Robert Gesell (physiology), Howard B. Lewis (biochemistry), Maurice H. Seevers, (pharmacology), and Walter J. Nungester and Malcolm H. Soule (bacteriology).

Professor Nungester, for example, made studies of pneumococci, discovering their existence in the blood stream, a pathway of infection not previously known. He demonstrated the limited effectiveness of serums and of certain of the body's immunizing processes. He made studies of the effect of mucin, the chief product of the mucous membrane, in lowering immunity. From his Rackham grants he bought a Tiselius electrophoresis apparatus, still in use, to make chemical analyses of parasitic virulence and the process of infection.

With assistance from the Horace H. Rackham Fund ($1,440, 1939–41), the United States Bureau of Entomology and Plant Quarantine, and the University's School of Forestry and Conservation, now called the School of Natural Resources, in which he is Professor of Economic Zoology, Samuel A. Graham investigated the hemlock borer's ravages in the woods of Michigan's Upper Peninsula. In 1949 he received a second Rackham research grant of $1,400 to make a controlled study of logging as a tonic for an aging swamp-forest near Imp Lake.

In 1951 Professor Frederick P. Thieme (anthropology) made a biological survey of the population of Puerto Rico ($1,950).

Psychological approaches to biology were early supported by grants from the Trustees of the Horace H. Rackham and Mary A. Rackham Fund. In June, 1935, they granted $1,400 to Professors Carl R. Brown and Burton D. Thuma (now Associate Dean of the College of Literature, Science, and the Arts) for studies in the psychological side of visual acuity. The Board of Governors continued support of the project from 1936 to 1938 with $1,500 from the Horace H. Rackham Fund. The findings were published.

The Trustees in 1934 and 1935 gave Professor Norman R. F. Maier $4,481.85 for his experiments with obfuscated rats, and the Board of Governors added $21,490, between 1936 and 1952, for a continuation of these experiments, since, in the words of Professor Maier, ". . . our work had been more fruitful than we had anticipated. It is because of our success in producing profound nervous breakdowns in animals that we have had to diverge rather than converge our efforts." Professor Maier and his associates contributed significantly to the knowledge of abnormal behavior, the processes of learning and memory under stress, and the relationships of brain cortex to attention and neurosis, and they stimulated similar work in a great many psychological laboratories. In 1939 *Life* magazine published several pages on Professor Maier's experiments, and this account prompted Mr. E. B. White to write for the *New Yorker* his classic story "The Door," now read by students in freshman English at the University.

Aided by a Rackham research grant of $1,945, Professor Edward L. Walker, a psychologist, in 1951 studied biologically the relationship of human drives and learning to the factors contributing to persistent avoidances in human behavior.

For some years, the Trustees of the Horace H. Rackham and Mary A. Rackham Fund had made direct grants to the biological laboratory on Barro Colorado Island, in the Canal Zone. In 1938 the Board of Governors began to contribute to the support of this biological station and continued its $300 yearly grants until 1946.

Language and Literature

Requests for Rackham research grants in language and literature have been few, compared to those in the sciences. In literary scholarship, the need for special equipment is negligible, the practicality of research assistance is limited, and the necessity for travel to foreign libraries has been greatly reduced by microfilms and bibliographies. Nevertheless, Rackham research grants in this field have totaled $100,686.88.

Two individual grants have added significantly to the holdings of the

University Library. In 1940 the Board of Governors assigned $4,000 to buy some thirteen thousand rare volumes of philosophy, literature, and economic history from the collection of Max S. Handman, Professor of Economics. Also in 1940 Joe Lee Davis, Professor of English, received $1,000 to pay for microfilming sixty-one sets of eighteenth-century American magazines, thus completing the Library's collection, one now unequaled anywhere. Several studies of American literary and cultural history have been based on this material.

Accomplishments in classical studies with the aid of Rackham research funds have been considerable. With a grant of $862.64 in 1939–40, Professor William H. Worrell was able to complete his already sizable card bibliography of publications pertaining to Coptic culture. Grants amounting to $20,980.80, between 1936 and 1942, brought research on the University's explorations at Karanis and Seleucia[53] to the point of publication. Under the direction of the University's Institute of Archeological Research, Professors Orsamus M. Pearl, John G. Winter, and Herbert C. Youtie studied and edited the papyri from Karanis, and Professor Clark Hopkins worked with the discoveries at Seleucia.

Three Rackham grants have done much to make the University a leader in linguistic studies. The smallest of these contributions ($3,600 in 1944–45) went to the University's English Language Institute, which is under the direction of Professor Charles C. Fries, for research and service in the teaching of English as a foreign language, particularly to students from Latin America and the Orient.

Grants totaling $7,343.44 (1938–52) went to Professor Albert H. Marckwardt for an analysis of the idiom of the Great Lakes states, an extension of the linguistic atlases sponsored by the American Council of Learned Societies, of which the one concerning New England and the one concerning the Atlantic Seaboard had been edited by Professor Hans Kurath, then of Brown University but since 1946 a member of the faculty of the University of Michigan. By June, 1952, Professor Marckwardt and his assistants had collected data by eight-hour interviews with 308 persons in 155 communities in Wisconsin, Illinois, Indiana, Ontario, and Ohio, and in the section of Kentucky along the south bank of the Ohio River. Scholars from several midwestern universities, assisted by grants from their own institutions, co-operated in the project. When completed the records will cover not only the characteristic speech of the differing neighborhoods throughout the area but such distinctive idioms as those of the Mennonite communities in Indiana and the German settlement around Frankenmuth, Michigan. A number of authoritative studies have already come from the project. Other universities are undertaking similar investigations in the upper Midwest, the lower Midwest, the Gulf States, the Rocky Mountain States, and the Pacific Coast, to complete the proposed comprehensive linguistic atlas of American English, of which Professor Kurath continues as editor.

Michigan's biggest accomplishment in linguistic scholarship is undoubtedly its *Middle English Dictionary,* which has received $62,900 from Rackham funds. In the 1930's, Professor Samuel Moore, an authority on Middle English dialects, outlined a dictionary of the English language from 1100 to 1475, the year when English printing began, and, as editor, started its compilation. Professor Moore was succeeded by Professor Thomas A. Knott, General Editor of Webster's New International Dictionary (second edition, unabridged), and his successor was Professor Kurath. The following statement appears in the first part of the *Middle English Dictionary,* which was published early in 1953:

> The compilation of the *Middle English Dictionary* has since 1930 been a project of the University of Michigan, supported by its own and contributed funds. The *Dictionary* is based on a collection of Middle English quotations which includes all those assembled for the Oxford Dictionary and in addition hundreds of thousands gathered by more than a hundred scholars who participated in a systematic reading program which covered all types of writings. The completed *Dictionary* will run to approximately 8,000 pages; it will be issued in 124-page parts, five or six a year, over a period of ten years.

The *Dictionary* will become a definitive key to the English culture of the Middle Ages.

The Social Sciences and Related Fields

Often before the social scientist can begin his analysis, particularly in certain fields, he must make surveys, conduct interviews and tests, and compile comprehensive data. For this preliminary work, he needs research assistants. The social scientist's laboratory is the city, the diplomat's office, or similar sources of information; in other words, his laboratory is the field, and he and his assistants must travel to it. Consequently, Rackham grants to the social sciences and related subjects have reached an impressive total of $236,239.49, comprising grants to the following departments, listed in the order of the amounts allocated: philosophy, geography, history, economics, political science, psychology, sociology, and anthropology. Grants have also been made, under this heading, for research in the fields of business administration and education, and for three interdepartmental projects: a broad area study of Germany, a program in Japanese studies, and an expedition to the Near East.

Philosophy

The single Rackham grant in philosophy, to Professor Roy W. Sellars ($715.20, 1946–47), is self-explanatory. Of his project to re-examine traditional materialism in the light of the relativity and quantum theories in physics, Professor Sellars wrote:

> I have written a great deal through the forty years I have been connected with the University but in the traditional fashion of sitting down and reading, thinking and writing. I should like to see whether a philosopher could get farther if he had a chance to talk things over with distinguished men in science particularly whose answers to this question might

throw light upon points. It is partly a semantic question, that is, a question of intelligent communication. I find that specialists and philosophers tend to speak different languages and these barriers ought to be broken down. And they can't be through letters and books alone.

Professor Sellars returned from his discussions, arranged by previous correspondence, to report that his peripatetic method was only partly rewarding and that the philosopher still did his most successful traveling in his mind.

Geography

Three geographers have carried out five projects, assisted by $7,010 in Rackham grants. In 1939 and 1940 Professor Preston E. James received $750 to compile and draft maps summing up his extended studies in Brazil. Professor George Kish received $1,000 in 1947 to locate and copy the oriental maps in the libraries of the Netherlands, Great Britain, France, Spain, and Portugal, in order to trace the influence of oriental mapmakers of the sixteenth, seventeenth, and eighteenth centuries on Western cartography. Between 1939 and 1942 Professor Kenneth C. McMurry received $5,260 to assist in three cartographical analyses of Michigan's public lands acquired through tax delinquency.

History

Four men have received a total of $8,421.85 for historical research. Professor Verner W. Crane was assisted by $221.93 (1938–39) in the studies which have made him a recognized authority on Benjamin Franklin. In 1948 Professor Howard M. Ehrmann received $1,450 to study the immediate origins and diplomacy of World War II, continuing his wide studies on the background of World War I.

The Cleveland Public Library turned over to the University in 1950 its sponsorship, along with its materials and completed editorial work, of the *Digest of the Red Archives.* The work to be done involved preparing a summary in English and an index for *Krasnyi Arkhiv,* papers published by the Central Archive Department of Russia that had remained without English translation and without index, even in Russian. The Cleveland Public Library had published a first volume, covering thirty of the 106 volumes of Archives that had appeared between 1922 and 1941. Since 1950, Professor Andrei A. Lobanov-Rostovsky has received $5,149.92 from Rackham funds to bring the *Digest* to completion.

In 1950 Professor William B. Willcox received $1,600 for research assistance in editing the two-volume manuscript, "History of the American Revolution," written by Sir Henry Clinton, principal commander of the British forces, a man curiously slighted by school books in favor of Howe, his early superior, and of Cornwallis, his subordinate. His handwritten history, now among Clinton's papers in the University's Clements Library, was clearly the most important Revolutionary document remaining unpublished. Professor Willcox's edition will soon be released by the Yale University Press.

Economics

Five studies in economics have been supported by $18,429.19 in Rackham money. Indeed, Rackham Research Project No. 1 (the first grant made by the Board of Governors for a new, as opposed to a continuing, research project) was Professor Charles F. Remer's investigation of the economic and social implications of commuting between Detroit and neighboring Windsor, across national borders. Both the United States and Canada were interested in the extent to which their working citizens traveled each day across the Detroit River. Professor Remer received a grant of $1,500 (May, 1936) for this project, and between 1938 and 1947, he also received grants amounting to $7,114.23 to study investments made by international entrepreneurs. Professor William Haber received $975 (1938–39) to study governmental policy and administration of unemployment relief, and Professor Z. Clark Dickinson received $2,039.96 (1937–41) to study collective wage bargaining. The results, in each case, were published. Perhaps the most impressive publication in economics assisted by Rackham money was that of Professor I. Leo Sharfman, who was designated "Rackham Professor in Economics" (1936–37), with the equivalent of his academic salary and relief from academic duties, in order to complete the final book of his five-volume report on the Interstate Commerce Commission, which, in 1930, the government had appointed him to prepare.

Political Science

A variety of projects in political science have received a total of $21,180.41.[54] Two were historical studies. Assisted by a grant of $800 (1947–48) for photostats and other materials, Professor Lionel H. Laing, at the request of the American Historical Association, is now editing the records of the Colonial Court of Vice-Admiralty of Boston. He has published previously on admiralty law and the importance of the Boston court in shaping this phase of American legal thinking. Assisted by a $2,000 Rackham grant, Professor James H. Meisel is in Italy this year collecting and studying the works of Gaetano Mosca, a somewhat neglected force in the history of totalitarian theory. Though Mosca's *The Ruling Class* is required reading in advanced political science classes, it is the only one of Mosca's works available in English, and Professor Meisel's forthcoming monograph on Mosca will undoubtedly be the first in any language.

Four projects have dealt with political systems: Professor Arthur W. Bromage studied central and local government in Ireland ($600, 1939–40); Professor John A. Perkins, state supervision over county governments in Michigan ($35.21, 1942–43); Professor John W. Lederle, provincial politics in

Canada ($850, 1945–46); and Professor James K. Pollock, parliamentary districts in Great Britain ($500, 1944–45).[55] Two current projects deal with political policy. Professor Lawrence Preuss, who served three years in the State Department and helped draft the United Nations Charter, is studying the political and legal problems connected with the Western European Union, an alliance outside the United Nations that was formed as a result of the wide use of the veto in United Nations proceedings; Professor Preuss's preliminary investigation was aided by a Rackham grant of $1,180 (1949–50). This year, Professor Russell W. Fifield, a former member of the United States Foreign Service in China and a subsequent traveler in southeast Asia, received a Rackham research grant of $2,500 to supplement a Fulbright grant awarded to enable him to study the foreign policies of the several new Asiatic nations, particularly their attitudes toward (a) their neighbors, (b) Nehru's India, (c) Mao's and Chiang's China, (d) postwar Japan, (e) Soviet Russia, and (f) their former colonial rulers.

Psychology

Eleven projects in psychological research have received a total of $23,675.20. In general, the work has concerned itself with devising laboratory controls and tests which can confirm, reject, or suggest scientific assumptions as to the workings of the mind and can measure personality. Professors Walter B. Pillsbury and George Meyer have worked with the processes of memory and with psychological diagnosis through memory tests. Professors Angus Campbell and Clyde H. Coombs have analyzed attitudes toward Russia; Professor Coombs has also explored a technique of measurement in the social sciences. Professor Edward S. Bordin has studied counseling processes; Professor Max L. Hutt, the methods and effectiveness of group psychotherapy. Professor E. Lowell Kelly has kept records over a span of twenty years on some three hundred married couples (starting with interviews just before marriage) to determine which combinations of personality endure, which fail, what changes of personality occur in marriage, and how such changes relate to marital success. Professors Daniel R. Miller and Gerald S. Blum have done significant work in phrasing and testing empirically some of the major assumptions of psychoanalysis. With Professor Guy E. Swanson, a sociologist, Professor Miller is now studying the way in which mental disorders relate to underlying social conditions, seeking the reason for preponderances in each social class of different mental diseases.

Sociology

Sociological research has been supported by $43,394.68 in Rackham money, and has included studies of transiency and migration in American cities, of leadership in city life, and of the basic assumptions made by socio-

logical analysts. The Board of Governors continued support, amounting to
$9,000 in 1936 and 1937, to Professor Lowell J. Carr's work in juvenile delin-
quency, begun under grants by the Trustees of the Rackham Fund. He was
also assisted by $13,879.68 in grants from the Board of Governors to complete
a study of "industrialization and cultural inadequacy" at the Willow Run
housing areas and trailer camps during the war, and a follow-up study of the
reintegration of the Willow Villagers after the industrial drive was over.[56] In
1952, with a grant of $2,690, Professor Carr began a study of the sociological
causes for the wide variation in numbers of criminal sex-offenders in different
Michigan counties.

Professor Horace M. Miner, with a Rackham grant of $2,300, went to
Morocco, in the summer of 1949, to study the effect of the basic personality
traits of a population on a total culture. Professor Miner used his previous
analysis of the Arabs of Timbuktu to determine the effect of Arab taboos and
traits on the cosmopolitan French culture of Morocco, working through detailed life histories and psychological tests of his informants.

Anthropology

Six anthropologists have received Rackham grants amounting to
$46,038.57. Professor Leslie A. White received $195 in 1940–41 to assist him in
collecting materials for a biography of Lewis H. Morgan (1818–81), who was
the virtual founder of American anthropology and whose thinking influenced
social science in Europe and Asia, as well. Professor Mischa Titiev made two
trips to Chile and Peru in 1941 and 1948 with the aid of $3,500 in Rackham
grants. He studied the impact of modern culture on the Araucanian Indians
of Southern Chile, a people who had resisted all invasions from the time of
the Incas until their communal lands were opened to colonization by the
Chilean government in 1928. At the same time Professor Titiev was also able
to make a study of Japanese settlements in Peru.

The remaining anthropological projects have dealt with Michigan. In
1935 the Horace H. Rackham and Mary A. Rackham Fund had given Professor Carl E. Guthe[57] $10,000 for his studies of the early Michigan Indian tribes.
Between 1936 and 1942 the Board of Governors continued support of Professor Guthe's excavations and research with a total of $28,251.11. This work was
closely associated with that of Dr. Wilbert B. Hinsdale, former Dean of the
University's School of Homeopathic Medicine, whose great interest in Indian
history led to his recognition as a leading authority in this field and to his
appointment, after retirement, as Honorary Curator in the Museum. Dr.
Hinsdale and Professor Emerson F. Greenman received $9,600 in Rackham
funds for additional work in Indian archeology (1938–45), which Professor
Greenman carried on after Dr. Hinsdale's death in 1944. Through these three
men, the University's Museum of Anthropology acquired an outstanding
Indian collection and added much to anthropological knowledge.

At two sites near Killarney, Ontario, Professor Greenman discovered remnants of a Stone-Age culture similar to that of northern Europe, throwing light on the first inhabitants of the New World. Geological surveys by Professor George M. Stanley[58] dated these relics at about 13,000 B.C. Indian history was greatly enhanced by Professor Greenman's analysis of the historical data on Michigan's Indians for the period between 1650 and 1760, which he secured from six extant answered questionnaires that had been circulated between 1820 and 1823 by Governor Cass of the Michigan Territory, and by a similar analysis of the answers to the same questions that Professor Greenman secured from the descendants of the Michigan tribes still living in Ontario, Wisconsin, Nebraska, Michigan, and Oklahoma.

In the summer of 1948, Professor James B. Griffin, assisted by a $2,492.46 grant, made a scientific excavation at a site north of Buchanan, Michigan, along the St. Joseph River, where the stratified evidence of over 500 years of Indian camping was threatened with damage from amateur excavators.

Business Administration

With a Rackham research grant of $3,550, the first to be made in the School of Business Administration, Herbert F. Taggart, Professor of Accounting and Assistant Dean of the School, is studying the legal defenses made by companies accused under the Robinson-Patman Act of selling their goods at overgenerous discounts to certain of their customers. The defenses seek to prove, as the act allows, that the manufacturers have sold for less only where production and shipping costs were less. With accounting sheets of great intricacy, the manufacturer attempts to show the Federal Trade Commission how much it cost to produce and market a pound of chicory, a pair of shoes, or a box of soda crackers. To the last penny the salaries of presidents and floor-sweepers, the mileage of salesmen and truckdrivers, the bills for coal and carbon paper, must all be reduced to production cost. Each company develops its own accounting sheets and presents its defense in its own way, some presentations running to eight thousand pages. Dean Taggart is making a historical study of these different ways of accounting and of presentation, to demonstrate, for future businessmen, lawyers, accountants, and economists, which methods succeed and which fail, which are valid and which erroneous.

Education

The Board of Governors has made four grants, totaling $13,164.59, to projects in education. It gave $8,103.75 to support an international conference, held in Ann Arbor during the summer of 1940, of the New Education Fellowship, an early attempt to consider, as the United Nations now does, the educational problems of the world. It gave $1,500 (1938–39) toward an analysis of the laboratory program in the University's Elementary School, a program in which the growing child is studied from a wide variety of aspects. Between 1943 and 1948 it assisted, with $939.57, Professor Edgar G. Johnson's study of the fragmentary education acquired by children of Spanish-speaking migrant workers in Michigan. Currently, the Board of Governors is aiding, with $2,000, the combined work of five Professors of Education: W. Robert Dixon, Edward J. Furst, Howard Y. McClusky, William C. Morse, and G. Max Wingo. Assuming two criteria of successful teaching—the ability to see things through the student's eyes and the ability to lead a group—these educators are refining and establishing tests of teacher competencies, empirical guides that are needed in the evaluation of teachers and teacher training.

German Area Studies

A significant development in social-science research since World War II has been the growth in interest in analyzing the culture of a particular area from as many academic viewpoints as can be brought to bear. One of the University's first ventures into these "area studies" was an inquiry into German National Socialism. This study, financed by a $12,000 grant from the Rockefeller Foundation, was begun in the War Seminar, an interdepartmental group organized July 1, 1941, with Professor Charles F. Remer, of the Department of Economics, in charge. Rackham research funds supported research growing out of this seminar with two $2,000 grants in 1942 and 1943, and with a $6,075 grant in 1945. The principal study, made by Dr. Helmut G. Callis, who held a doctor's degree in economics from the University of Leipzig, dealt with the totalitarian concept of international relations. Under the direction of Professor Harlow J. Heneman (political science), a study of German labor under National Socialism was also made.

A regional project of somewhat wider scope was conducted by Professors James K. Pollock[59] (political science), Willett F. Ramsdell (forestry), and William C. Trow (educational psychology), with the assistance of grants, in 1944 and 1947, amounting to $9,200. Combining their particular skills, the members of this group surveyed the states and provinces of Germany for their "social, economic, political, and cultural customs, activities, and beliefs." These analytical interpretations of life in each district were printed in booklets by the United States Military Government for American officers and civilians serving in post-Nazi Germany. The booklets received high praise, and Professor Pollock and his associates have recently recast them into a single, authoritative volume.[60]

The Center for Japanese Studies

Another of the University's "area" studies likewise grew out of the war. The University had trained a large number of experts on Japan for military and governmental service, and after the war, in order to benefit from these scholars and enhance the University's program in Far Eastern studies, Professor Robert B. Hall, Department of Geography, proposed the Center for Japanese Studies, which he now directs. On April 25, 1947, the Regents accepted a gift of $125,000 from the Carnegie Corporation to support the Center for the first five years, the Board of Governors of the Horace H. Rackham School of Graduate Studies agreeing to provide $6,000 a year in Rackham money. This obligation was assumed by the University's general funds in 1952.

The Center aims to make its studies of Japan from many points of view. The Departments of Anthropology, Economics, Fine Arts, Geography, History, Japanese Language and Literature, Political Science, and Sociology participate. Graduate students may enroll in the program and carry on work toward the Ph.D. degree; they are required to fulfill the degree requirements of their particular departments, as well as the requirements of the Center, which are extensive. The student must first earn the master's degree in Far Eastern Studies (Japanese area) and must participate in the Center's research seminar in Ann Arbor. He must complete a year's field work at the Center's station in Okayama City, Japan—a large Japanese house, with adjoining dormitory and tennis court, well equipped with statistical machines, tape-recorders, and jeep station wagons. Here he does his own doctoral work and assists in the general research of the Center, which is, in essence, an extended study of Western influence on Japan.

At the University, the Center maintains a library of 50,000 volumes, files of twenty-three Japanese scientific periodicals, and an excellent collection of maps. The Japanese Ambassador to the United States dedicated the Center in 1952, and it was visited on September 22, 1953, by H.I.H., Crown Prince Akihito.

Expedition to the Near East

Invited by both Iran and Iraq, Professor George G. Cameron, then Chairman of the Near Eastern Committee of the Social Science Research Council, organized, raised money for, and directed the University of Michigan Near Eastern Expedition of 1951. Toward the total cost of $26,100, the Board of Governors granted $8,100 from Rackham research funds.

The expedition consisted of Professors George G. Cameron (historian and archeologist), Douglas D. Crary (geographer), and N. Marbury Efimenco (political scientist), and graduate students John Anderson (zoologist), Carter Zeleznik (historian and archeologist), Ernest McCarus (linguist), William Masters (anthropologist), and Joel Canby (medical student and biologist). They traveled through Beirut, Baalbek, and Damascus to establish headquarters in Baghdad, and from there up through Azerbaijan, and down to Kermanshah. They took impressions of hitherto undeciphered, bilingual inscriptions on three stone pillars (one at an altitude of 10,000 feet, in ice and mountain wind) that promise to unlock lost languages of the past.

This ancient country of the Medes and Persians, swept over by Alexander and ruled by Rome, is today a point of tension between Russia and the West. The members of the expedition studied its past and present with a thoroughness stimulated by their combined interests. The project was productive of results in all fields, and the University's position in Near Eastern studies was greatly strengthened. Excerpts from Professor Cameron's reports are illustrative:

> In Kuwait, Efimenco, the political scientist, concentrated on administrative procedure; his success was viewed as phenomenal by residents long established there. Crary, the geographer, and Masters, the anthropologist, then entered the important but relatively unknown areas inhabited by the marsh and swamp Arabs; the information they secured was equally outstanding.
> Almost literally, in Iraq and Iranian Kurdistan, we have left no stone unturned, no archeological site or modern town unexplored, no discipline untouched. At the same time, we have settled down long enough in the Rowanduz area, in one spot, to get more than a fair picture of a very typical community.

The Fine Arts

During the first twelve years, the Board of Governors received but two requests, and made no grants, for research in the fine arts. Since 1948, however, it has granted a total of $11,864.49 to six researchers.

Professor Theodore Larson, School of Architecture and Design, received assistance amounting to $1,580.71 (1951–52) to analyze the fundamentals of design for university library buildings. After consulting librarians and photographing libraries in several parts of the country, Professor Larson is now preparing a series of large cards which will show graphically the underlying needs, both functional and environmental, in university library construction.

Professor Harold E. Wethey, Department of Fine Arts, received $1,164 (1948–49) to study the work of Alonso Cano, a neglected Spanish artist and craftsman of the seventeenth century. Professor Wethey traveled to Spain to find and photograph Cano's paintings, sculptures, and buildings. Most of Cano's work had never been photographed; many items had been wrongly attributed to him; much remained unrecognized. With evidence collected in Spain, France, and England, Professor Wethey is now reconstructing Cano's artistic career.

Professor Carl D. Sheppard, Department of Fine Arts, received $1,219.78 (1949–50) to assist him in tracing, through Sicily and Southern Italy, a little-known classic revival in sculpture and architecture which flourished under the Norman king, Frederic II (1220–50). Starting with two pulpits in Salerno, dated by inscriptions but redecorated during the revival, Professor Sheppard established connections between the great Norman cathedral at Monreale, Sicily, and what proved to be earlier and later work on the mainland at Campania and Capua. He took pictures of carvings, churches, and castles. He also looked for traces of Palestinian and Byzantine art incorporated by returning First Crusaders in their Sicilian monuments.

Professor Louise E. Cuyler, School of Music, received $2,000 (1948–49) for research on the masses of Heinrich Isaac, a Flemish musician whose *Choralis Constantinus* had been published in Austria in 1555. An Austrian musical society had begun publishing this work in modern notation, but the second World War put an end to its project. Professor Cuyler, after visiting libraries in London, Brussels, Constance, and Munich, was able to complete the work, publishing Book III of Isaac's *Choralis*.[61] This year, Professor Cuyler received a second grant of $2,000 toward further work on Isaac and toward a history of the music of the Low Countries.

Professor Percival Price, University Carillonneur, received a grant of $1,500 (1949–50) to extend his earlier work on European bells,[62] which had been made with assistance from the Faculty Research Fund and the Niagara Falls Bridge Commission. Studying logbooks and manufacturers' records, as well as the carillons themselves, Professor Price made a survey of wartime wreckage and confiscation of European carillons.

Assisted by a grant of $2,400 (1952–53), Mrs. Kamer Aga-Oglu, Associate Curator in the University's Museum of Anthropology and Lecturer in Anthropology, has recently completed a tour from Scandinavia to Turkey to further her research on oriental porcelains. For ten years Mrs. Aga-Oglu had been working with the Museum's collection of about eight thousand pieces of this rare china, which had been brought back by the Philippine expedition that had been financed, anonymously, by Mr. Rackham.[63] It is the largest collection of excavated pieces in the world and includes scarce Chinese, Siamese, and Japanese porcelains and other little-known Asiatic wares from the tenth to the nineteenth centuries. They had been imported into the Philippines and suggest a great deal about the early commercial and cultural traffic between those islands and the mainland. Mrs. Aga-Oglu has restored, from fragments, a very large number of the best pieces, and on her recent tour she took with her several specimens and many photographs, which she discussed with the experts in the countries she visited. There she also took pictures and made measurements of pieces in museums and private homes, studying especially the collection of 10,000 whole pieces in the old Ottoman Imperial Palace in Istanbul. Her study will be published in four volumes. The first, *Chinese Blue and White Porcelain,* is now nearly completed.

The Health Sciences

Charged by Mr. Rackham's will to promote the welfare of mankind, the Trustees of the Horace H. Rackham and Mary A. Rackham Fund gave large sums to the University for research connected with human health. Their million-dollar endowment of the Rackham Arthritis Research Unit and their specific grants in 1934 and 1935, listed earlier, show their recognition of medical research as important in the alleviation of human misery. The Board of Governors has continued to support medical research and has made grants to the health sciences totaling $307,372.85, an amount exceeded only by those assigned to the physical and biological sciences. In ascending order, the grants are divided into the following categories: public health, dentistry, pediatrics, neuropsychiatry, surgery, medicine.

Public Health

Research in Public Health has received a total of $4,383.90. In 1945, with a grant amounting to $1,148.45, Professor Odin W. Anderson began a study of health services for the aged, then being pioneered in the state of Washington. The fact that the number of citizens reaching old age was increasing rapidly and the further fact that the Social Security Board was then considering grants to the states for care of the aged, gave the survey particular timeliness. In 1951, assisted by $1,235.45, Professor Richard J. Porter began a search for the improved detection of intestinal amoebae, because, under the microscope, the one common harmful amoeba looks much like its innocuous relatives. This research is still going forward. Assistance from Rackham research funds, however, was not continued because support was forthcoming from other sources. Dr. Pearl L. Kendrick ($2,000, 1953–54) is making a study of immunity in pertussis (whooping cough).

Dentistry

In addition to the $26,996.30 granted to Drs. Bunting and Jay to continue the work on dental caries earlier supported by grants from the Rackham Trustees,[64] the Board of Governors has assigned $12,100 to dental research. Dr. Floyd A. Peyton received $4,000 (1949–51) for an investigation of the heat generated by dental drilling instruments. Dr. George R. Moore received $8,100 (1938–44) for a study of the relationship between heredity and malocclusion, a study making possible certain corrections of bad bite in children by foreseeing, from their heredity, the future development of tooth, jaw, and facial structure.

Pediatrics

From 1939 to 1941, $5,100 in Rackham money assisted Drs. D. Murray Cowie (pediatrics) and John H. Ferguson (pharmacology) in their search for unknown factors in blood coagulation that are related to hemophilia and similar diseases in children. After Dr. Cowie's death in 1940, Dr. Ferguson went on to publish a number of articles describing their findings, including a new theory of blood coagulation. Drs. Ernest H. Watson and George H.

Lowery made extensive studies of the development of glands and of preconscious sexual behavior in children ($8,437.40, 1948–51). Drs. Donald A. Sutherland and James L. Wilson studied the lower alimentary canal in children and infants ($2,510.38, 1950–51). Altogether, the total granted for research in pediatrics was $16,047.78.

Neuropsychiatry

Grants totaling $25,676.68 have assisted clinical investigations of the brain and nerves. Drs. Basu K. Bagchi and Robert C. Bassett ($1,600, 1944–50) clarified the electrical diagnosis of brain tumors by thoroughly correlating electroencephalographic signs with the differing tumors indicated. Dr. Konstantin Scharenberg ($6,915, 1947–50) investigated the gray matter of the brain, carrying on the work of Del Rio Hortega, who had died in 1945, after discovering, in his Buenos Aires laboratory, the structures which support neural ganglia. Dr. Scharenberg also collaborated with Dr. Raymond R. Waggoner ($6,030, 1940–47) in a systematic study of the thalami (the junctions between the brain and nerves) in idiocy. Using experimental animals, Drs. Russel N. DeJong and Elizabeth C. Crosby[65] ($8,600, 1952–53) investigated the effects of nerve injury.

Two psychiatric studies have been made. With a grant of $406.73 (1940–47) Dr. Ralph M. Patterson investigated the relationship between emotional stress and heart beat, a clue to psychosomatic disorders; by using a radio-thermometer he attained measurements more accurate than those formerly possible. Drs. Ralph D. Rabinovitch[66] and Sara Dubo studied the psychic effects of mother love in infancy ($2,124.95, 1950–52); from psychiatric evaluations and childhood records of adults orphaned at an early age, they established the significance of "mothering" during the first two years of life.

Surgery

Under grants totaling $8,321.62 (1949–51), four surgeons investigated the extent to which lung tissue can be safely removed in pulmonary diseases. Drs. John Alexander and Edgar P. Mannix analyzed exhaled breath and the air absorbed by the blood to determine human respiratory capacity in cases of removal of lung tissue; Drs. Cameron Haight and W. Burford Davis, in conjunction with the University's Heart Station,[67] experimented directly with animals to discover the effects of lung removal on the lesser circulatory system. With a grant of $3,000 (1953–54) Dr. Robert E. L. Berry is exploring the extent to which surgery can go in eradicating stomach cancers. Dr. Frederick A. Coller's researches were assisted, in 1935, by $3,800 from the Rackham Trustees and, until 1946, received continuing support from the Board of Governors, totaling $40,040. His research resulted in numerous publications on the chemistry, treatment, and postoperative care of patients injured by crushing, shock, or burning. In all, support to surgery from the Horace H. Rackham Fund has amounted to $51,361.62.

Medicine

Various medical studies have received, altogether, $170,806.57. The $3,000 granted by the Rackham Trustees, in 1934, covered the treatment of forty-two indigent syphilitics[68] during 478 hospital days and led to grants amounting to $3,500 from the Board of Governors (1937–40) for continued treatment and laboratory experiment under the supervision of Dr. Udo J. Wile. The Rackham Trustees in 1934 and 1935 gave $6,200 to Dr. Louis H. Newburgh for research in metabolism, and the Board of Governors supported with $60,564.84 (1936–45) his further extensive studies in this field that established him as an authority on obesity, especially in relation to diabetes. They also supported for five years ($10,820, 1939–43) another study in the chemistry of the human body: the investigation by Dr. Henry Field of various aspects of nutrition, which gained additional support from the Upjohn Company. A third extended research program, in which, as in the case of Dr. Newburgh's work, the Board of Governors followed up an initial grant by the Rackham Trustees ($5,000, 1934), was that of Dr. Frank N. Wilson in the University Hospital's Heart Station. The $20,962.50 which the Board granted Dr. Wilson between 1936 and 1944 was augmented by payments from the Lincoln National Life Insurance Company for analyses of electrocardiograms. Dr. Wilson's work in the Heart Station was nationally recognized as early as 1938, by the establishment, with contributions from all over the country, of the Dr. Frank Norman Wilson Lectureship in Cardiography. In 1945 the Kresge Foundation gave the University $50,000 to support fellowships at the Heart Station for a ten-year period.

Four other studies have dealt with aspects of the heart and blood system. Dr. Warren K. Wilner investigated the functioning of the heart under anesthesia ($4,297.50, 1950–51); Dr. Richard H. Lyons developed data concerning changes in the size of the heart and blood vessels as the relative volumes of body fluids alter ($5,655.24, 1942–46); Dr. Otto T. Mallery studied the *Rh* blood factor ($1,745, 1949–50); Dr. Arthur C. Curtis investigated the relationship of carotene—a red hydrocarbon—to the fats and other ethereal esters, a relationship important to an understanding of diabetes.

Two studies have concerned themselves with specific diseases. To determine the incidence of tuberculosis among doctors, nurses, and hospital workers, Dr. John B. Barnwell sought out hundreds of persons formerly connected with the University Hospital, tracing medical students and nurses through the alumni catalogue. He made examinations and collected reports covering information on many health questions and recorded his findings on I.B.M. cards. Some of his findings were used by a congressional committee on labor.

His grants totaled $6,270 (1940–46). Dr. Albert H. Wheeler ($3,550, 1953–54) is studying immunology by comparing the resistance of mice to natural and to induced tumors.

A number of studies have dealt with physiological relationships. Dr. Henry K. Schoch ($3,737.66, 1951–52) studied the abnormal conduct of diseased kidneys; Dr. Newburgh ($2,600, 1945–46) studied the reabsorption of sodium in kidney diseases; and Dr. Tommy N. Evans ($3,000, 1953–54) is studying change in kidney function in normal and toxemic pregnancies. Relationships between the thyroid and the ovaries and between the thyroid and the adrenal glands were studied by Dr. William H. Beierwaltes ($6,133.89, 1949–51). Dr. Norman F. Miller ($3,760, 1937–45) made a series of studies of the importance of the endocrine glands in gynecology and obstetrics, particularly in cancer of the cervix. Dr. Jerome W. Conn ($4,500, 1945–46) studied the causes of hypoglycemia, a deprivation of blood-sugar which results in dizziness and other physical and mental disturbances and may even result in death. Interested in this deprivation among nursing mothers, Dr. Conn disproved the established belief that loss of sugar in the blood was brought about as the breasts converted blood into milk and suggested, instead, that excessive activity of the anterior pituitary gland, known to be connected with lactation, was the root of the disease. With a grant amounting to $883.11 (1949–50) Dr. Muriel C. Meyers analyzed the cellular structure of bone marrow to establish criteria for its growth; she published several articles on leukemia.

Studies have been made in drugs: by Dr. John D. Adcock on antibiotics and chemotherapy ($6,000, 1945–47); by Dr. Chris J. D. Zarafonetis on the clinical uses of para-aminobenzoic acid ($866, 1949–50); and by Dr. Ivan F. Duff and his associates on various anticoagulants ($4,900, 1949–53).

Rackham Publications

An important adjunct to the research program supported by grants from the Horace H. Rackham Fund is the allotment for the publication of research and scholarly work known as the Rackham Publication Fund.

Publication is essential to the researcher and to the effective use of his results. It is true that the press of his university may publish his books and that the journals of his profession may publish his articles, but such scholarly publication sometimes must be subsidized, because some professional journals cannot afford to print, without a grant of money, essential extra pages, plates, or diagrams. Moreover, the university presses, such as that of the University of Michigan, although designed specifically to help finance the publication of scholarly works, do not have unlimited funds and so cannot accept all faculty manuscripts, however worthy of publication. Nor does the relatively small demand for books in highly specialized fields justify their acceptance by the commercial publishing houses.

With these facts in mind, on April 25, 1938, the Board of Governors set aside $12,000 to support publication during the year 1938–39, carrying out, again, the letter of Mr. Rackham's will. No general allotment was made the following year, but by the end of 1939–40 specific grants for publication during the first two years had totaled $13,254, and beginning with 1940–41, approximately $8,000 yearly was made available. Altogether, through 1952–53, the Board of Governors granted $105,699.27 for publication.

A list of the publications that have been aided by the Fund will be found in Appendix IV. They may be summarized by fields, as follows: physical sciences, 7 (2 books); natural sciences, 44 (11 books); social sciences, 31 (29 books); language and literature, 16 books; fine arts, 3 books; health sciences, 9 (3 books.) Receipts from sales of publications are applied toward repayment of the original grant or are used to assist other publication.

Grants for articles range from twenty to thirty dollars for extra pages to several hundred dollars for illustrations. A Rackham grant of $150, for example, paid for twenty-four of the twenty-six microphotographic pictures illustrating Dr. Konstantin Scharenberg's study of the cerebellum by the silver techniques of the Spanish school, the first ever presented in print;[69] a grant of $380 permitted reproduction of two paintings by George M. Sutton, professor and naturalist, illustrating his studies of the whippoorwill and the vesper sparrow.

Grants from the Publication Fund, ranging from $200 to more than $3,000, have assisted in the production of a number of distinguished books. The two volumes on papyri and ostraca from Karanis, the work of Professors Orsamus M. Pearl, Herbert C. Youtie, and John G. Winter, illustrate well the wide discrepancy between intrinsic and monetary values in scholarly publication. These were the last two of twelve volumes on papyrology in the University's Humanistic Series, summing up the University's almost unequaled collection that had resulted from Mr. Rackham's early personal support of Professor Kelsey's work. When the Egyptian government had permitted removal of the documents to Ann Arbor, it had been with the provision that University scholars would edit and print them. Printing in Greek characters, however, is expensive, as is the work involved in marking conjectural readings, bracketing, and footnoting; representative pictures of original texts also add materially to the cost. For these reasons, the cost of publication came to about fourteen dollars a volume. The demand from the general public for such costly and specialized books is limited, and although the University's agreement with other universities to exchange all scholarly publications brings valuable volumes to the University Library, it does not bring money to the Business Office. It was the Rackham Publication Fund that made possible the completion of this carefully prepared and finely printed series.

Even a brief description of the books listed in Appendix IV will not be attempted here, but a few of the more unusual ones should perhaps be mentioned. James B. Griffin's *Archeological Survey in the Lower Mississippi Alluvial Valley 1940–47* is an authoritative work on the Midwestern Indians. Federico Sanchez y Escribano's *Cosas y Casos* brings together, for the first time, texts from the everyday life of the Spain in which Cervantes and Lope de Vega lived. Morris P. Tilley's *A Dictionary of the Proverbs in England in the Sixteenth and Seventeenth Centuries* is a standard reference work. Harold Wethey's *Colonial Architecture and Sculpture in Peru* received a citation from the Society of Architectural Historians as "the most distinguished volume by an architectural historian" for the year 1949.

In all, $1,440,010.97 in Rackham grants has been spent for research and publication. This figure does not include grants made by the Trustees of the original Horace H. Rackham and Mary A. Rackham Fund but only the grants made by the Board of Governors of the Horace H. Rackham School of Graduate Studies from the income of the endowment of the Graduate School that became the Horace H. Rackham Fund.

The record shows that the administration of the funds has been both frugal and productive. In general, the individual grants have been relatively small, but in many cases, and certainly in the aggregate, they have resulted in tremendous additions to knowledge. At the same time, interest and activity in all fields of scholarship and research have been stimulated, and here, perhaps, may lie an ultimate and continuing value as important as that of the more tangible results. For a university lives by the intellect; the intellect lives only by continued examination and re-examination of man and the universe. By perpetually seeking to satisfy his intellectual curiosity the researcher keeps alive his highest faculty and carries to his students respect for the human mind and a sense of intellectual discipline which may well outlast the facts of the course he is teaching. If the intellectual life is more valuable than the physical, if its products last longer, if, indeed, it is the measure of a civilization, then, in the continuing program of research at the University of Michigan, Horace H. Rackham's fortune is well serving mankind.

Appendix I

Rackham Gifts to the University

(compiled from the *Proceedings of the Board of Regents*)

1922–1941

Summary

1922–33	From Horace H. Rackham	$ 605,000.00
1936–40	From Mary A. Rackham	2,000,000.00
1935–40	From the Trustees of the Horace H. Rackham and Mary A. Rackham Fund	9,669,081.85
	Total	$12,274,081.85

Itemized List

FROM HORACE H. RACKHAM

1922	Greek Biblical manuscripts	$ 15,000.00
1922–25	Anthropological expedition to Philippines	30,000.00
1922–26	Three fellowships in creative arts	15,000.00
1922–30	Near East excavations and research (including purchase of Greek and Coptic papyri and Arabic and Persian calligraphy)	445,000.00
1933	Loans and gifts to undergraduate students (by bequest)	100,000.00

FROM MARY A. RACKHAM

1936	Endowment of Institute for Human Adjustment	1,000,000.00
1939 & 1940	Horace H. Rackham Educational Memorial (University of Michigan's share)	1,000,000.00

FROM THE TRUSTEES OF THE
HORACE H. RACKHAM AND MARY A. RACKHAM FUND

	Buildings		$ 3,075,000.00
1935	Horace H. Rackham School of Graduate Studies	$2,500,000.00	
1936	Institute for Human Adjustment	75,000.00	
1939	Horace H. Rackham Educational Memorial ...	500,000.00	
	Endowments		6,000,000.00
1935	Horace H. Rackham Fund	4,000,000.00	
1937	Rackham Arthritis Research Fund	1,000,000.00	
1938	Horace H. Rackham Fund for Undergraduate Scholarships	100,000.00	
1938	Rackham Sociological Research Fund	500,000.00	
1941	Addition to Horace H. Rackham Fund for benefit of Institute for Human Adjustment	400,000.00	

	Grants for Expenses		305,000.00
1936	Horace H. Rackham Fund	100,000.00	
1937	Institute for Human Adjustment	100,000.00	
1938	Rackham Sociological Research	5,000.00	
1940	Institute for Human Adjustment	100,000.00	
	Fellowships		13,500.00
1934	10 fellowships of $1,000 each	10,000.00	
1935	7 fellowships of $500 each	3,500.00	
	Faculty Research Grants		219,881.85
1934	Astronomy in South Africa	6,000.00	
1934	Research into cancer of the eye (Dr. Laura A. Lane)	2,500.00	
1934	Research at the University Heart Station (Dr. Frank N. Wilson)	5,000.00	
1934–35	Excavations in Egypt	50,000.00	
1934–35	Research into juvenile delinquency (Professor Lowell J. Carr)	12,000.00	
1934–35	Research into dental caries (Dr. Russell W. Bunting)	20,000.00	
1934–35	Research by the Bureau of Reference and Research in Government	24,000.00	
1934–35	Research into brain psychology (Dr. Norman R. F. Maier)	4,481.85	
1934–35	Research into metabolism (Dr. Louis H. Newburgh)	6,200.00	
1935	Research into infantile paralysis	5,000.00	
1935	Research into rickets (Dr. Coral A. Lilly)	1,500.00	
1935	Michigan Indian History (Dr. Carl E. Guthe and Dr. Wilbert B. Hinsdale)	10,000.00	
1935	Research in surgery (Dr. Frederick A. Coller)	3,800.00	
1935	Research, at the Fresh Air Camp, into juvenile delinquency (Professor Lowell J. Carr)	18,000.00	
1935	Research into visual acuity (Professors Carl R. Brown and Burton D. Thuma)	1,400.00	
1935	Nuclear research and the building of a cyclotron (Professor Harrison M. Randall)	25,000.00	
1935–36	Construction of a solar tower at the McMath-Hulbert Observatory, Lake Angelus, Michigan	25,000.00	
	Miscellaneous Grants		55,700.00
1934	Hospitalization of needy, expectant mothers	15,000.00	
1934	Hospitalization and treatment of indigent syphilitics	3,000.00	
1934	Construction of a therapeutic swimming pool ...	20,000.00	
1934	Purchase of books for the FERA Freshman College Program	2,500.00	
1934	Conducting a class in lip reading	200.00	
1935	Establishing graduate social-work training in Detroit	10,000.00	
1935	Postgraduate teaching of physicians in rural areas	5,000.00	

Appendix II
Chronology

June 13, 1933.	The death of Horace H. Rackham.
July 17, 1933.	The Law School receives Mr. Rackham's law library.
September 30, 1933.	President Ruthven confers with the Trustees of the Horace H. Rackham and Mary A. Rackham Fund.
October 20, 1933.	The University receives, as provided by Mr. Rackham's will, $100,000 for the Horace H. Rackham Loan Fund for undergraduate students.
January 1, 1934.	The Horace H. Rackham and Mary A. Rackham Fund becomes operative.
March 26, 1935.	President Ruthven proposes a gift from the Horace H. Rackham and Mary A. Rackham Fund of $5,000,000 for a Horace H. Rackham School of Graduate Studies.
August 28, 1935.	Discussions and correspondence begin, leading to the establishment, later, of the Institute for Human Adjustment.
September 7, 1935.	The University receives $5,000,000 for the building and endowment of the Horace H. Rackham School of Graduate Studies.
November 1, 1935.	The Trustees add $1,500,000 to the $1,000,000 already designated for the Graduate School building and site.
April 27, 1936.	The Board of Governors of the Horace H. Rackham School of Graduate Studies holds its first meeting.
June 11, 1936.	Mrs. Rackham gives the University $1,000,000, inaugurating the Institute for Human Adjustment.
June 19, 1936.	The Trustees authorize the University to provide a building for the Institute for Human Adjustment, with an expenditure up to $75,000.
December 30, 1936.	The Board of Governors approves the Speech Clinic as the first unit of the Institute for Human Adjustment.
June 17, 1937.	The $1,000,000 Rackham Arthritis Research Fund is established.
February 28, 1938.	The Board of Governors accepts an assignment of $25,000 from the unused portion of the $75,000 building grant of June, 1936, for the purchase of a building to house the Psychological Clinic as part of the Institute for Human Adjustment.
February 28, 1938.	The Trustees give $100,000 for Rackham Undergraduate Scholarships.
May 1, 1938.	The Rackham Sociological Research Unit is established and endowed with $500,000; it becomes part of the Institute for Human Adjustment.
June 17, 1938.	The Horace H. Rackham School of Graduate Studies is dedicated.
July 29, 1938.	The Fenton Community Center is endowed with $100,000.
December 2, 1938.	The University receives an additional $35,000 for the Fenton Community Center.
March 27, 1939.	The University receives $500,000 from Mrs. Rackham for the Horace H. Rackham Educational Memorial, in Detroit.
May 11, 1939.	The University receives an additional $500,000 for the Horace H. Rackham Educational Memorial from the Rackham Trustees.
January 26, 1940.	The University receives $10,000 additional for the Fenton Community Center.

January 29, 1940.   Mrs. Rackham gives $750,000 for additional land for the Horace H. Rackham Educational Memorial, $500,000 of which was later determined to be the University's share.

December 31, 1941. The University receives from the Trustees $400,000 for the Horace H. Rackham Fund, the income to be earmarked for the Institute for Human Adjustment.

January 28, 1942.   The Horace H. Rackham Educational Memorial is presented to the University of Michigan and the Engineering Society of Detroit.

January 2, 1946.   The University of Michigan Fresh Air Camp is placed within the Institute for Human Adjustment.

July 10, 1950.   The Board of Trustees of the Horace H. Rackham and Mary A. Rackham Fund dissolves.

June 4, 1951.   The Division of Gerontology is established under the Institute for Human Adjustment.

Appendix III

Projects Assisted by Rackham Research Grants

(I) THE PHYSICAL SCIENCES

1. Bachmann, Werner E. (chemistry)
   The synthesis of sex hormones and of antimalarials (1939–49) ... $ 15,700.00
2. Bartell, Floyd E. (chemistry)
   Study of free surface energies (1936–47) 7,659.85
3. Blicke, Frederick F. (pharmaceutical chemistry)
   (a) Antispasmodics (1939–40) 200.00
   (b) Study of synthetic substitute for ergot (1942–43) 4,000.00
4. Brockway, Lawrence O. (chemistry)
   (a) Construction of electron diffraction outfit for research on
       molecular structure (1939–40) (see Schoepfle) 950.00
   (b) Construction of mass spectrograph (1941–42) 2,500.00
   (c) Structural research on a series of new compounds
       for possible war uses (1943–44) 1,250.00
   (d) Purchase of electron diffraction unit for solids (1943–44) 7,500.00
5. Brownell, Lloyd E. (chemical and metallurgical engineering)
   Fluid flow through porous media (1949–50) 1,400.00
6. Case, Ermine C. (geology)
   Collection of vertebrate fossils in central Montana (1938–39) 2,000.00
7. Case, Lee O., and Alfred L. Ferguson (chemistry)
   Redetermining the standards of measurement for
   electrolytic conductivity (1936–37) 2,655.00
8. The Cyclotron, Nuclear Research (1936–49) 141,514.06
9. Dow, William G. (electrical engineering)
   Investigation of space charge and transit time at
   ultra-high frequencies (1941–43) 743.72
10. Eardley, Armand J. (geology)
    Tertiary geology of the basins north of Great Salt Lake (1945–46) 150.00
11. Eardley, Armand J., and Thomas S. Lovering (geology)
    Studies of geological processes by means of models (1938–39) 1,418.80
12. Electron Microscope (1941–45) 44,322.49
13. Fajans, Kasimir (chemistry)
    Dispersion of light, and the electronic structure
    of molecules (1941–48) 17,149.86
14. Ferguson, Alfred L. (chemistry) (see Case, Lee O.)
    A thorough and critical study of the literature on electrochemical
    polarization and overvoltage (1949–51) 4,900.00
15. Glaser, Donald A. (physics)
    Investigation on cosmic ray mesons (1950–51) 1,500.00
16. Gordy, Charles B. (mechanical engineering)
    Study of variation in muscular movement pattern with changes in
    speed of same operator (1945–46) 111.62

17. Great Lakes Research Institute
    Pleistocene history of Great Lakes (1947–50) 7,500.00
18. Harary, Frank (mathematics)
    Applications of mathematics to social psychology
    and statistical mechanics (1953–54) 1,600.00
19. Hazen, Wayne E. (physics)
    Study of interactions of cosmic rays and nuclei (1948–49) 2,500.00
20. Heinrich, E. William (mineralogy)
    Investigation of the internal structure of
    European pegmatites (1949–50) 1,510.00
21. Hibbard, Claude W. (geology)
    Study of Pleistocene and Cenozoic vertebrates (1951–53) 5,016.00
22. Hoad, William C. (civil engineering)
    Studies in the disposal of city garbage with city sewage (1940–41)   317.65
23. Housel, William S. (civil engineering)
    Research on soil mechanics (1939–47) 1,751.25
24. Johnston, Bruce G. (civil engineering)
    Design and analysis of steel frames under atomic blast (1952–53)   3,000.00
25. Katz, Donald L. (chemical and metallurgical engineering)
    (a) Bibliography of phase equilibria under high pressure (1940–41) ..   800.00
    (b) Electron-microscopic studies of oils and industrial solids (1942–46)   4,200.00
26. Kellum, Lewis B. (geology)
    Studies in Mexico (1936–42) 2,372.86
27. Lake Angelus Observatory
    To complete a tower for taking motion pictures of the stars (1937)   5,000.00
    For an assistant astronomer (1936–39) 5,900.00
28. Lamont-Hussey Observatory
    Astronomical studies in South Africa (1942) 25,054.85
29. Landes, Kenneth K. (geology)
    (a) Investigation of ground water supplies by
        electrical resistivity methods (1942–43) 500.00
    (b) Geology of Mackinac Straits region (1943–44) 896.19
    (c) Geology of southeastern Michigan and adjoining areas (1946–47)   1,535.00
30. Lovering, Thomas S. (geology) (see Eardley)
31. McLaughlin, Dean B. (astronomy)
    (a) A comparative study of the spectra of novae (1939–40) 200.00
    (b) Studies of peculiar and variable stellar spectra (1941–42) 500.00
32. Maugh, Lawrence C. (civil engineering)
    Study of the structural action of various types
    of rigid joints (1939–40) 950.43
33. Meyer, Charles F. (physics)
    Modification of Twyman and Green interferometer (1938–39) ...   395.75
34. Nierenberg, William A. (physics)
    Fundamental particles of physics (1949–50) 2,500.00
35. Randall, Harrison M. (physics)
    Applications of infrared spectroscopy to
    biological research (1949–50) 3,000.35
36. Rondestvedt, Christian S., Jr. (chemistry)
    Mechanism of arylation by free radical generators (1953–54) 4,000.00

37. Sawyer, Ralph A. (physics), and Raymond W. Waggoner (psychiatry)
    Methods of analysis for lead in biological materials (1938–39) 1,000.00
38. Schoepfle, Chester S. (chemistry)
    Electron diffraction studies (1938–39) 1,200.00
39. Scott, Irving D. (geology)
    Coastal dunes and postglacial history of Lake Michigan (1942–43)   2,000.00
40. Sinnott, Maurice J. (chemical and metallurgical engineering)
    The effect of oxygen on the austenite grain size of steel (1948–49)   634.59
41. Smith, Peter A. S. (chemistry)
    Synthesis of nitrogen heterocycles by means of aryl azides (1949–50)   2,869.00
42. Stanley, George M. (geology)
    (a) Study of late Pleistocene shorelines in Hudson Bay (1939–40) 700.00
    (b) Study of later postglacial beaches near
        Killarney, Ontario (1940–41) 240.00
    (c) Varve and peat study to determine age of
        glacial Lake Algonquin (1945–46) 754.26
43. Thomassen, Lars (chemical and metallurgical engineering)
    (a) Structure of protective coatings on magnesium alloys (1942–46) ..   3,003.20
    (b) Geiger-Counter X-ray spectrometer (1945–46) 5,500.00
44. Upthegrove, Clair E. (chemical and metallurgical engineering)
    Nitrogen in steel (1942–43) 76.43
45. Van den Broek, Jan A. (engineering mechanics)
    Studies in lines of force and elasticity (1938–43) 1,223.04
46. Vaughan, Wyman R. (chemistry)
    Sterochemistry of replacement of functional groups
    by hydrogen (1951–52) 3,300.00
47. Vincent, Edward T. (mechanical engineering)
    Research on the combustion of oil-burning engines (1940–43) ...   558.25
48. White, Alfred H. (chemical engineering)
    (a) Researches on Portland cement (1940–41) 500.00
    (b) Studies in magnesium alloys and the
        pyrolysis of hydrocarbons (1942–45) 2,885.75
49. Williams, Neil H. (physics)
    The production and absorption of extremely short
    electromagnetic waves (1938–39) 750.00
50. Williams, Robley C. (astronomy)
    The distribution of energy in infrared stellar spectra (1945–46) ..   550.00
51. Wood, William P. (metallurgical engineering)
    Effect of alloying elements on the austenite
    transformation in cast iron (1940–41) 500.00

                                      $ 366,870.25

(II) The Biological Sciences

1. Bailey, Reeve M. (zoology)
   Faunal affinities of the endemic fish fauna of the Green River
   system, Kentucky and Tennessee (1953–54) 1,900.00
2. Barro Colorado Biological Laboratory (1939–46) 2,400.00

3. Bartlett, Harley H. (botany)
    Ethnobotany of the Hampangan-Mangyan and
    Tagbanau of the Philippines (1947–48) 1,000.00
4. Baxter, Dow V. (forest pathology and botany)
    Control of Alaskan wood-destroying fungi and
    of decay in western red cedar (1951–53) 3,500.00
5. Baylor, Edward R. (zoology)
    Comparison of the physiological factors of growth and
    light production of bacteria (1950–52) 3,400.00
6. Bernthal, Theodore G. (physiology)
    The role of the carotid body in the control of blood flow (1939–40)   863.00
7. Blair, W. Frank (zoology)
    The rate of dispersal of the deer-mouse *(Peromyscus maniculatus*
    blandus) between areas of different soil color (1939–40) 425.00
8. Brassfield, Charles R. (physiology)
    Comparison of changes in the pH of arterial blood and saliva
    with the glass electrode (1939–40) 500.00
9. Brodkorb, Pierce, and Norman Hartweg (zoology)
    Ornithological and herpetological survey of the
    Sierra Madre of Chiapas (1940–41) 1,350.00
10. Brown, Carl R., and Burton D. Thuma (psychology)
    Visual acuity (1936–38) 1,600.00
11. Brown, Dugald E. S. (zoology)
    Actomyosin contraction at high pressure (1951–52) 3,500.00
12. Burt, William H., and Norman E. Hartweg (zoology)
    A biological survey of the area around Paricutin, Mexico (1945–46)   2,450.00
13. Burt, William H., and Laurence C. Stuart (zoology)
    Zoological explorations in Alta Verapaz, Guatemala (1939–40) ... 1,450.00
14. Cain, Stanley A. (natural resources)
    Preparation of a *Pollen Atlas* (1951–54) 3,846.40
15. Clover, Elzada U. (botany)
    (*a*) Botanical exploration in unknown areas of
    Utah and Arizona (1938–39) 300.00
    (*b*) A botanical study of tropical, desert areas with special reference to
    the cactaceae and similar desert types (1946–47) 1,600.00
16. Crosby, Elizabeth, and Russell T. Woodburne (anatomy)
    Morphological and experimental study of the
    primate nervous system (1938–53) 23,313.33
17. Dice, Lee R. (zoology)
    Studies of aging and human heredity (1940–49) 80,093.23
18. Eckstein, Henry C. (biochemistry)
    Lipotropic action of amino acids (1944–46) 2,040.00
19. Eggleton, Frank E. (zoology)
    (*a*) Geddes Pond limnological investigation (1940–41) 500.00
    (*b*) Biology of the Sphaeriidae (1944–45) 600.00
20. Elliott, Alfred M. (zoology)
    Studies on the physiology of the protozoa (1947–52) 5,670.00
21. Gesell, Robert (physiology)
    Reflexogenic components of respiratory rhythm
    and the mechanisms of nerve cells (1940–51) 9,000.00

22. Graham, Samuel A. (economic zoology)
    (a) Hemlock borer study (1939–41) 1,440.00
    (b) Decadence of mature white spruce on the Imp Lake area (1948–49) 1,400.00
23. Gustafson, Felix G. (botany)
    Studies in the fertilization, growth and
    chemistry of plants (1937–54) 9,222.27
24. Halvorson, Harlyn O. (bacteriology)
    Studies on the mechanism of protein synthesis in yeast (1952–53) 3,000.00
25. Hartweg, Norman E. (zoology) (see Brodkorb, and Burt)
26. Hooper, Emmet T. (zoology)
    (a) A proposed expedition to the Guadalupe Mountains (1939–40) .. 497.63
    (b) Evolution, ecology, and geographic distribution
    of harvest mice (1947–50) 2,900.00
    (c) Ecological distribution of the species of
    tree squirrels of Mexico (1952–53) 2,500.00
27. Hooper, Frank F. (zoology)
    Ecology of the microscopic fauna of the
    mud-water interface (1951–52) 661.60
28. Hubbell, Theodore H. (zoology)
    Index-catalogue to the literature on the
    Orthoptera of the New World (1947–49) 4,623.56
29. Hubbs, Carl L. (zoology)
    (a) Analysis of speciation and the genetics of
    systematic characters in fishes (1937–38) 500.00
    (b) Fishes of the desert (1942–43) 1,450.00
    (c) Acclimatization and use of mosquito fish
    to control malaria in Michigan (1943–45) 2,099.82
30. Kemp, Norman E. (zoology)
    Studies of genesis in the yolk of frogs' eggs (1947–51) 3,341.18
31. Lagler, Karl F. (zoology and natural resources)
    (a) Fishes of the islands in Michigan waters
    of the Great Lakes (1945–46) 1,600.00
    (b) Ichthyology of the Porcupine Mountain
    region of Michigan (1948–49) 1,275.00
32. La Rue, Carl D. (botany)
    Studies of growth and reproduction in plants (1939–54) 14,400.00
33. Lawrence, W. S. (pharmacology)
    Chemotherapy of paragonimiasis (1945–46) 959.75
34. Lewis, Howard B. (biochemistry)
    (a) Study of the biochemistry and the
    detoxication of selenium (1938–39) 350.00
    (b) The intermediary metabolism of the naturally occurring sulfur-con-
    taining amino acids, cystine and methionine (1939–43) 2,787.27
    (c) Chemical factors in lathyrism (1943–46) 3,399.16
    (d) The intermediary metabolism of thiourea,
    thiouracil and related compounds (1946–47) 1,080.00
    (e) Lathyrism and other food intoxications due to legumes (1948–49) 1,800.00
    (f) Nutritive value of B-lactoglobulin; influence of heat on its
    biological properties (1949–50) 1,201.00

35. Lundell, Cyrus L. (botany)
    A study of the vegetation of the Yucatan Peninsula (1938–39) ...   1,000.00

36. Maier, Norman R. F. (psychology)
    Studies of the brain, and of abnormal behavior
    in the rat (1936–52) 21,490.00

37. Miller, Lila (biochemistry) (*see* Pollard, under Health Sciences)

38. Miller, Robert Rush (zoology)
    Speciation in viviparous fishes of the genus *Poeciliopsis*
    in northwestern Mexico (1953–54) 2,500.00

39. Moe, Gordon K. (pharmacology)
    Action of drugs on myocardial automaticity and impulse (1945–46)   1,800.00

40. Nanney, David L. (zoology)
    Studies in protozoan genetics (1951–52) 1,800.00

41. Nungester, Walter J. (bacteriology)
    Studies of experimental pneumonia (1937–46) 14,081.67

42. Seevers, Maurice H. (pharmacology)
    Effects of morphine and related substances on
    intermediary metabolism (1942–43) 830.20

43. Smith, Frederick E. (zoology)
    The effect of environmental deficiency upon
    population growth (1951–52) 1,672.67

44. Soule, Malcolm H. (bacteriology)
    Studies of bacteria and spirochetes; cultivation of acid-fast organ-
    isms; production of purified proteins (1937–51) 20,926.58

45. Sparrow, Frederick K. (botany)
    A monograph on the aquatic phycomycetes (1938–39) 498.94

46. Steere, William C. (botany)
    (*a*) Preparation of a manual and revision of the
    "Hepaticae of Michigan" (1938–39) 200.00
    (*b*) Studies in American mosses (1939–49) 3,748.32

47. Stockard, Alfred H. (zoology)
    The ontogeny of the muscles and their nerve supply
    in the domestic pig (1947–48) 505.24

48. Stuart, Laurence C. (zoology) (*see* Burt)
    Herpetology in Guatemala (1945–49) 4,100.00

49. Taylor, William Randolph (botany)
    Marine algae of Pacific waters (1948–49) 1,199.78

50. Thieme, Frederick P. (anthropology)
    Biological survey project on the Puerto Rican population (1950-51)   1,950.00

51. Thuma, Burton D. (psychology) (*see* Brown, Carl R.)

52. van der Schalie, Henry (zoology)
    (*a*) Geographic and ecological survey of
    terrestrial mollusks of Michigan (1938–40) 510.00
    (*b*) The origin and relationships of fossil fresh-water mussels
    to present mussel fauna (1942–43) 350.00
    (*c*) Basic studies of groups of snails serving as
    vectors in schistosomiasis (1952–54) 4,400.00

53. Walker, Edward L. (psychology)
    (a) Drive specificity and learning (1948–49) 1,394.31
    (b) Factors contributing to the persistence of
        avoidance behavior (1952–53) 1,945.00
54. Whitaker, Wayne L. (anatomy)
    Studies on rats with portal vein ligation or
    porto-caval anastomosia (1946–47) 925.71
55. Woodburne, Russell T. (anatomy) (see Crosby)
56. Woodhead, Arthur E. (zoology)
    The life-history cycle of the giant kidney worm (1940–51) 4,000.00
57. Wright, Paul A. (zoology)
    (a) Photoelectric estimation of melanin dispersion
        in excised frog skin (1947–48) 2,360.11
    (b) Studies in the properties of intermedin (1949–52) 3,300.00

$ 311,277.73

(III) Language and Literature

1. Davis, Joe Lee (English)
    Studies in 18th century American magazines (1939–40) 1,000.00
2. The English Language Institute (1944–45) 3,600.00
3. The Handman Library
    To buy the library of Professor Max Sylvius Handman (1940–41)   4,000.00
4. The Institute of Archeological Research
    Editing papyri found at Karanis, and studies of the
    excavations at Karanis and Seleucia (1936–42) 20,980.80
5. Marckwardt, Albert H. (English)
    A survey of the folk speech of the Great Lakes region
    and the Ohio River Valley (1938–53) 7,343.44
6. The Middle English Dictionary (1946–54) 62,900.00
7. Worrell, William H. (Oriental languages and literatures)
    A bibliography of Coptic studies (1939–40) 862.64

$ 100,686.88

(IV) The Social Sciences and Related Fields

1. Angell, Robert C. (sociology)
    Leadership as a factor in the integration of cities (1947–48) 10,000.00
2. Blum, Gerald S., and Daniel R. Miller (psychology)
    The psychoanalytic theory of orality:
    an experimental approach (1949–50) 1,901.54
3. Bordin, Edward S. (psychology)
    The development of a multivariate analysis
    of counseling processes (1949–50) 2,699.79
4. Bromage, Arthur W. (political science)
    Central and local government in Ireland (1939–40) 600.00
5. Cameron, George G. (Near-Eastern studies)
    University of Michigan Near-Eastern expedition (1950–51) 8,100.00
6. Campbell, Angus, and Clyde Coombs (psychology)
    A factor analysis of attitudes toward Russia (1947–48) 916.39

7. Carr, Lowell J. (sociology)
    (*a*) Studies of juvenile delinquency (1936–38) 9,000.00
    (*b*) Study of adjustment at Willow Run (1943–51) 13,879.68
    (*c*) Study of the factors behind the distribution
        of sex offenses in Michigan (1951–52) 2,690.00
8. The Center for Japanese Studies (1948–51) 24,000.00
9. Coombs, Clyde (psychology) (*see* Campbell)
    A theory and technique of measurement
    for the social sciences (1950–51) 2,430.82
10. Crane, Verner W. (history)
    Studies of Benjamin Franklin (1938–39) 221.93
11. Dickinson, Z. Clark (economics)
    Investigation in the field of collective wage determination (1937–41) 2,039.96
12. Dixon, W. Robert, with Edward J. Furst, Howard Y. McClusky,
    William C. Morse, and G. Max Wingo (education)
    A study of two aspects of teacher competence (1952–53) 2,000.00
13. Ehrmann, Howard M. (history)
    A study of the immediate origins and diplomacy
    of World War II (1949–50) 1,450.00
14. Fifield, Russell N. (political science)
    Foreign policy in southwest Asia (1952–53) 2,500.00
15. Freedman, Ronald (sociology) (*see* Hawley)
    Population mobility in metropolitan areas (1953–54) 1,475.00
16. Greenman, Emerson F. (anthropology) (*see* Hinsdale)
    Archeological field work on Manitoulin Island (1939–46) 9,600.00
17. Griffin, James B. (anthropology)
    Archeological research in southwest Michigan (1948–49) 2,492.46
18. Guthe, Carl E. (anthropology)
    Michigan Indian history (1936–42) 28,251.11
19. Haber, William (economics)
    The administration of unemployment compensation (1938–39) .. 975.00
20. Hawley, Amos H., and Ronald Freedman (sociology)
    Selectivity of migration in Michigan, 1940–45 (1947–48) 2,000.00
21. Hinsdale, Wilbert B., and Emerson F. Greenman (anthropology)
    Michigan Indian history (1938–39) 2,000.00
22. Hutt, Max L. (psychology)
    Group psychotherapy: process, themas, outcome (1952–54) 5,500.00
23. James, Preston E. (geography)
    Compilation and drafting of maps of Brazil (1939–41) 750.00
24. Janowitz, Morris (sociology)
    Theoretical research into contemporary institutions (1952–53) .. 2,050.00
25. Johnston, Edgar G. (education)
    The educational status of children of migratory workers (1943–44) 939.57
26. Kelly, E. Lowell (psychology)
    The prediction of marital adjustment (1951–52) 2,000.00
27. Kish, George (geography)
    A study of Oriental influence on
    Western cartography, 1500–1800 A.D. (1947–48) 1,000.00
28. Laing, Lionel H. (political science)
    Editing the Colonial Vice-Admiralty Reports of Boston (1947–48) 800.00

29. Lederle, John W. (political science)
    The Canadian party system (1945–46) 850.00
30. Lobanov-Rostovsky, Andrei A. (history)
    Digest of Krasnyi Arkhiv (1951–53) 5,149.92
31. McMurry, Kenneth C. (geography)
    Delinquent taxes and land policy in Michigan (1939–43) 5,260.00
32. Meisel, James H. (political science)
    A study of Gaetano Mosca (1953–54) 2,000.00
33. Meyer, George (psychology)
    Development and standardization of some diagnostic
    memory tests for the clinical field (1938–41) 666.40
34. Miller, Daniel R. (psychology), and Guy E. Swanson (sociology)
    Social classes and related psychological differences (1951–54) 4,170.00
35. Miner, Horace (sociology)
    Basic personality structure and culture change (1949–50) 2,300.00
36. The New Education Fellowship
    A conference in Ann Arbor (1940) 8,103.75
37. Newcomb, Theodore M. (psychology)
    A panel of informants representative
    of the Michigan population (1946–47) 3,140.26
38. Olson, Willard C., and associates (education)
    The growth of the child as a whole (1938–39) 1,500.00
39. Perkins, John A. (political science)
    State administrative supervision over
    county governments in Michigan (1942–43) 35.21
40. Pillsbury, Walter B. (psychology)
    Study of retroactive effect of similar and
    disparate learning on immediate memory (1939–40) 250.00
41. Pollock, James K. (political science)
    Studies of the British electorate (1944–45) 500.00
42. Pollock, James K. (political science), Willett F. Ramsdell (forestry),
    and William C. Trow (educational psychology)
    German state and provincial research (1947–48) 9,200.00
43. Preuss, Lawrence (political science)
    The right of collective self-defense
    and the United Nations charter (1949–50) 1,180.00
44. Ramsdell, Willett F. (forestry) (*see* Pollock)
45. Remer, Charles F. (economics)
    (*a*) Study of "commuting" between Detroit and Windsor (1936–37) .. 1,500.00
    (*b*) Study of international capital movements (1938–47) 7,114.23
46. Sellars, Roy W. (philosophy)
    Materialism in the light of relativity and emergence (1946–47) ... 715.20
47. Sharfman, I. Leo (economics)
    Relief from other duties to complete last volume of five-volume
    report on U. S. Interstate Commerce Commission (1936–37) 6,800.00
48. Smith, Harold D. (political science)
    Bureau of Reference and Research in Government (1936–37) 12,000.00
49. Swanson, Guy E. (sociology) (*see* Miller)
50. Taggart, Herbert F. (business administration)
    Cost defenses under the Robinson-Patman Act (1953–54) 3,550.00

51. Titiev, Mischa (anthropology)
    The changing pattern of Araucanian culture (1941–49) 3,500.00
52. Trow, William C. (educational psychology) (*see* Pollock)
    A quantitative study of major interest areas
    of high-school students (1940–41) 621.27
53. War Seminar (interdepartmental)
    The origins of national socialism (1942–46) 10,075.00
54. White, Leslie A. (anthropology)
    Collecting materials for a biography of
    Lewis H. Morgan (1818–1881) (1940–41) 195.00
55. Willcox, William B. (history)
    Editing Sir Henry Clinton's manuscript history
    of the American Revolution (1949–50) 1,600.00

                                                          $ 236,239.49

(V) The Fine Arts

1. Aga-Oglu, Mrs. Kamer (anthropology)
   Special studies on Far-Eastern ceramics in the museums and private
   collections in England, Sweden, Holland, Belgium, France, and
   Turkey (1952–53) 2,400.00
2. Cuyler, Louise E. (music)
   (*a*) Scholarly edition of the masses of
   Heinrich Isaac (*ca.* 1450–1517) (1948–49) 2,000.00
   (*b*) A history of Low-Country music, and publication
   of sacred works of Heinrich Isaac (1953–54) 2,000.00
3. Larson, C. Theodore (architecture)
   Analysis of design requirements for university libraries (1951–52)   1,580.71
4. Price, Percival (music)
   Campanology (1949–50) 1,500.00
5. Sheppard, Carl D. (fine arts)
   Classicism in Romanesque sculpture of the
   Norman Kingdom of southern Italy (1949–50) 1,219.78
6. Wethey, Harold E. (fine arts)
   Alonso Cano, (1601–1667),
   painter, sculptor, and architect (1948–49) 1,164.00

                                                          $ 11,864.49

(VI) The Health Sciences

1. Adcock, John D. (internal medicine)
   Antibiotics and chemotherapy (1945–47) 6,000.00
2. Alexander, John, and Edgar P. Mannix, Jr., (surgery)
   Exploration of the physiological factors determining human respir-
   atory capacity in relation to borderline decompensation (1949–51)   7,961.68
3. Anderson, Odin W. (public health)
   Study of health services for recipients of
   old age pensions, Washington (state) (1945–46) 1,148.45
4. Bagchi, Basu K. (psychiatry), and Robert C. Bassett (surgery)
   Electroencephalographic and clinicopathological
   investigation of intercranial tumors (1949–50) 1,600.00

5. Barnwell, John B. (internal medicine)
   A study of the incidence of tuberculosis
   among hospital personnel (1940–46) 6,270.00
6. Bassett, Robert C. (surgery) (*see* Bagchi)
7. Beierwaltes, William H. (internal medicine)
   Thyroid-ovarian and thyroid-adrenal relations (1949–51) 6,133.89
8. Berry, Robert E. L. (surgery)
   A study of the mode of spread of cancer of the stomach with critical
   evaluation of present day operations for such lesions (1952–53) .. 3,000.00
9. Bunting, Russell W. (dentistry)
   Dental caries (1936–38) 19,000.00
10. Coller, Frederick A. (surgery)
    Chemical abnormalities of the sick surgical patient (1936–46) 40,040.00
11. Conn, Jerome W. (internal medicine)
    Acclimatization research (1945–46) 4,500.00
12. Cowie, D. Murray (pediatrics), and John H. Ferguson (pharmacology)
    The study of phospho-lipids in blood plasma in relation to blood
    coagulation in the hemorrhagic diseases of children (1939–41) .. 5,100.00
13. Crosby, Elizabeth C. (anatomy), and Russell N. DeJong (neurology)
    Experimental production of lesions within the
    primate central nervous system (1952–53) 8,600.00
14. Curtis, Arthur C. (internal medicine)
    (a) Experimental work to answer the problem of carotenemia in
    diabetes and to determine the relationship of carotene to
    high blood lipids (1940–41) 1,500.00
    (b) Studies in vitamin A metabolism (1941–42) 1,500.00
15. Davis, W. Burford (surgery) (*see* Haight)
16. DeJong, Russell N. (neurology) (*see* Crosby)
17. Dennis, Edward W. (internal medicine) (*see* Duff)
18. Dubo, Sarah (psychiatry) (*see* Rabinovitch)
19. Duff, Ivan F., with Edward W. Dennis and James W. Linman
    (internal medicine)
    Studies in anticoagulant drugs (1949–53) 4,900.00
20. Evans, Tommy N. (obstetrics and gynecology)
    A study of changes in renal function during
    normal and toxemic pregnancies (1952–53) 3,000.00
21. Ferguson, John H. (pharmacology) (*see* Cowie)
22. Field, Henry (internal medicine)
    Studies on nutrition (1939–44) 10,820.00
23. Haight, Cameron, and W. Burford Davis (surgery)
    Pathophysiologic observation on the effects of varying degrees of
    pulmonary resection on the cardiopulmonary system (1949–50) .. 359.94
24. Jay, Philip (dentistry)
    Dental caries research (1940–43) 7,996.30
25. Kendrick, Pearl L. (public health)
    Immunity studies in pertussis: the effect of
    specific antiserum on the infected chick embryo (1952–53) 2,000.00
26. Lane, Laura A. (ophthalmology)
    Study of cancer of the eye as an occupational disease (1936–40) ... 4,565.00

27. Linman, James W. (internal medicine) (*see* Duff)
28. Lowrey, George H. (pediatrics) (*see* Watson)
29. Lyons, Richard H. (internal medicine)
    Studies on the relationship between circulation
    and the blood volume (1942–46) 5,655.24
30. Mallery, Otto T. (internal medicine)
    Rh Hapten (1949–50) 1,745.00
31. Mannix, Edgar P., Jr. (surgery) (*see* Alexander)
32. Meyers, Muriel C. (internal medicine)
    In vitro studies of the cellular physiology of bone marrow (1949–50)   883.11
33. Miller, Norman F. (obstetrics and gynecology)
    Endocrine studies in gynecology (1937–45) 3,760.00
34. Moore, George R. (dentistry)
    A correlated study of heredity in relation to malocclusion (1938–44)   8,100.00
35. Newburgh, Louis H. (internal medicine)
    (*a*) Studies in metabolism (1936–46) 60,564.84
    (*b*) Readsorption of sodium by diseased kidneys (1945–46) 2,600.00
36. Patterson, Ralph M. (psychiatry)
    Psychosomatic relationships (1940–41) 406.73
37. Peyton, Floyd A. (dentistry)
    Heat developed during operation of
    revolving dental instruments (1949–51) 4,000.00
38. Pollard, H. Marvin, and Lila Miller (internal medicine and
    biological chemistry)
    A study of pancreatic function
    by the use of purified secretin (1939–40) 1,000.00
39. Pollard, H. Marvin (internal medicine)
    Studies of stomach and intestinal disease (1941–51) 8,495.83
40. Porter, Richard J. (public health)
    Studies on laboratory diagnosis of amebiasis (1950–51) 1,235.45
41. Rabinovitch, Ralph D., and Sara Dubo (psychiatry)
    The influence of the primary mother-child relationship
    on later personality growth (1950–51) 2,124.95
42. Scharenberg, Konstantin (psychiatry) (*see* Waggoner)
    Investigation of the Nissl-Gray substance of the brain (1947–50)   6,915.00
43. Schoch, Henry K. (internal medicine)
    Factors involved in the formation of edema (1951–52) 3,737.66
44. Sutherland, Donald A. (pediatrics) (*see* Wilson, James L.)
45. Waggoner, Raymond W., and Konstantin Scharenberg (psychiatry)
    (*see* Sawyer, under Physical Sciences)
    Neuropathologic investigation of idiocy (1940–47) 6,030.00
46. Watson, Ernest H., and George H. Lowrey (pediatrics)
    Endocrine studies in children (1948–51) 8,437.40
47. Wheeler, Albert H. (dermatology and syphilology)
    Immunologic studies of resistance to induced and
    spontaneous tumors in tissue-treated mice (1953–54) 3,550.00
48. Wile, Udo J. (dermatology and syphilology)
    (*a*) Syphilis treatment (1937–40) 3,000.00
    (*b*) Cultivation of the spirocheta pallida
    microorganism of syphilis (1939–40) 500.00

49. Wilner, Warren K., Jr. (anesthesiology)
     Investigation of cardiac function during anesthesia (1951–52) 4,297.50
50. Wilson, Frank N. (internal medicine)
     Heart station (1936–43) 20,962.50
51. Wilson, James L., and Donald A. Sutherland (pediatrics)
     A study of gastrointestinal tract physiology
     in infants and children (1950–51) 2,510.38
52. Zarafonetis, Chris J. D. (internal medicine)
     Study of clinical applications of
     para-amino-benzoic acid (1949–50) 866.00

$ 307,372.85

Grand total $1,334,311.69

Appendix IV

Books and Articles Supported by the Rackham Publication Fund

(I) THE PHYSICAL SCIENCES

1. Ayres, William L., and Raymond L. Wilder (eds.) (mathematics). *Lectures in Topology; the University of Michigan Conference of 1940* (Ann Arbor: University of Michigan Press, 1941), vii+316 pp.
2. Goldberg, Leo (ed.) (astronomy). *The Structure of the Galaxy* (Ann Arbor: University of Michigan Press, 1951), 84 pp.
3. Laporte, Otto, and J. E. Mack (physics). "The Spectrum of Neutral Tungsten," *Physical Review*, 63 (1943), pp. 246–97.
4. Losh, Hazel M. (astronomy). "Distribution of Sun-Spots in Longitude," *University of Michigan, Publications of the Observatory*, 7, No. 5 (1938), pp. 127–45.
5. McLaughlin, Dean B. (astronomy). "The Spectrum of Nova Persei 1901," *University of Michigan, Publications of the Observatory*, 9, No. 3, (1949), pp. 13–71.
6. Randall, Harrison M., with R. A. Oetjen (physics). "The Infra-red Spectra of the Isometric Octanes in the Vapor Phase," *Review of Modern Physics*, 16, Nos. 3 and 4, (1943), pp. 265–70.
7. Sawyer, Ralph A., with J. R. Platt (physics). "New Classifications in the Spectra of AuI and AuII," *Physical Review*, 60 (1941), pp. 866–76.
8. Williams, Robley C. (astronomy). "Spectrophotometric Determinations of Stellar Temperatures. I. The Color Temperature of Alpha Lyrae," *University of Michigan, Publications of the Observatory*, 7, No. 4, (1938), pp. 93–123.

(II) THE NATURAL SCIENCES

1. Baxter, Dow V. (forest pathology). (*a*) "The Effect of Cultural Practices Upon Disease Prevention and Control in American Plantations" (accepted for publication, University of Michigan Press). (*b*) "The Distribution and Occurrence of the Resupinate Polypores of North America" (accepted for publication, University of Michigan Press). (*c*) "Some Resupinate Polypores from the Region of the Great Lakes" (a series of papers, 1 through 25 to date, published in *Papers of the Michigan Academy of Science, Arts, and Letters*, or as *Contributions from the School of Forestry and Conservation, University of Michigan*, 1927–   ).
2. Blair, W. Frank (zoology). (*a*) "An Estimate of the Total Number of Beachmice of the Subspecies Peromyscus polionolus leucocephalus, Occupying Santo Rosa Island, Florida," *American Naturalist*, 80 (1946), pp. 665–68. (*b*) "Populations of the Deer-Mouse and Associated Small Mammals in the Mesquite Association of Southern New Mexico," *Contributions from the Laboratory of Vertebrate Biology, University of Michigan*, 21 (1943), 40 pp.
3. Burt, William H. (zoology). *The Mammals of Michigan* (Ann Arbor: University of Michigan Press, 1946), xv+288 pp.
4. Clover, Elzada U., and Lois Jotter (botany). "Floristic Studies in the Canyon of the Colorado River and Tributaries," *American Midland Naturalist*, 32 (1944), pp. 591–642.
5. Dansereau, Pierre (botany). (*a*) "Classification of Vegetation upon a Structural Basis," *Ecology*, 32, No. 2 (1951), pp. 172–229. (*b*) "The Varieties of Evolutionary Opportunity," *Revue Canadienne de Biologie*, XI (1952), pp. 305–88.

6. Dice, Lee R. (zoology), (a) "Variation in the Cactus-Mouse," *Contributions from the Laboratory of Vertebrate Genetics, University of Michigan,* 8 (1939), 27 pp. (b) "Variation in the Deer-Mouse," *Occasional Papers, Museum of Zoology, University of Michigan,* 375 (1938), 19 pp. (c) "Variation in the Wood Mouse," *Contributions from the Laboratory of Vertebrate Genetics, University of Michigan,* 9 (1939), 16 pp. (d) "Variation of Peromyscus Maniculatus in Parts of Western Washington and Adjacent Oregon," *Contributions from the Laboratory of Vertebrate Biology, University of Michigan,* 44 (1949), 34 pp.

7. Ehlers, George M., with E. C. Stumm and R. V. Kesling (geology). *Devonian Rocks of Southeastern Michigan and Northeastern Ohio* (Ann Arbor: Edwards Brothers, 1951), 40 pp.

8. Hooper, Emmet T. (zoology). "A Systematic Revision of the Harvest Mice (Genus Reithrodontomys) of Latin America," *Miscellaneous Publications of the Museum of Zoology, University of Michigan,* 77 (1952), 255 pp., 9 pls., 24 figs.

9. Hubbs, Carl L., with Laura C. Hubbs and R. E. Johnson (zoology). "Hybridization in Nature Between Species of Catostomid Fishes," *Contributions from the Laboratory of Vertebrate Biology, University of Michigan,* 22 (1943), 69 pp.
Hubbs, Carl L. (zoology). "Fishes from the San Carlos Mountains, Tamaulipas," *University of Michigan Studies, Science Series,* 12 (1937), pp. 293–97.
Hubbs, Carl L., and C. L. Turner (zoology). "Studies of the Fishes of the Order Cyprinodontes. XVI. A Revision of the Goodeidae," *Miscellaneous Publications of the Museum of Zoology, University of Michigan,* 42 (1940), 85 pp., 5 pls.

10. Liljeblad, Emil (zoology). "Monograph of the Family Mordillidae (Coleoptera) of North America, North of Mexico," *Miscellaneous Publications of the Museum of Zoology, University of Michigan,* 62 (1945), 229 pp. 7 pls.

11. Lundell, Cyrus L. (botany). (a) "Studies in American Celastraceae—I," *Bulletin of Torrey Botanical Club,* 65 (1938), pp. 463–76. (b) "Revision of the American Celastraceae," *Contributions from the University of Michigan Herbarium,* 3 (1939), 46 pp. 10 pls. (c) "Studies of Tropical American Plants—I," *ibid.,* 4 (1940), 32 pp. (d) "Studies of American Spermatophytes—I," *ibid.,* 6 (1941), 66 pp., 5 illus. (e) "Studies of American Spermatophytes—II," *ibid.,* 7 (1942), 56 pp. (f) "Flora of Eastern Tabasco and Adjacent Mexican Areas," *ibid.,* 8 (1942), 95 pp., 4 pls.

12. Mains, Edwin B. (botany). "Rusts from British Honduras," *Contributions from the University of Michigan Herbarium,* 1 (1939), pp. 5–19.

13. Miller, Robert R. (zoology). "The Cyprinodont Fishes of the Death Valley System of Eastern California and Southwestern Nevada," *Miscellaneous Publications of the Museum of Zoology, University of Michigan,* 68 (1948), 155 pp., 5 figs., 15 pls., 3 maps.

14. Smith, Alexander H. (botany). (a) "Notes on Agarics from British Honduras," *Contributions from the University of Michigan Herbarium,* 1 (1939), pp. 21–28. (b) "Studies in the Genus Cortinarius—I," *ibid.,* 2 (1939), 42 pp. (c) "Studies of North American Agarics—I," *ibid.,* 5 (1941), 73 pp., 32 pls.

15. Snyder, Marshall L. (bacteriology). "A Simple Colorimetric Method of Estimation of Relative Numbers of Lacto-bacilli in the Saliva," *Journal of Dental Research,* 19 (1940).

16. Sparrow, Frederick K. (botany). *The Aquatic Phycomycetes* (Ann Arbor: University of Michigan Press, 1943), xx+785 pp.

17. Steere, William C. (botany). (a) Papers published in *The Bryologist* (1942). (b) *Liverworts of Southern Michigan* (Bloomfield Hills, Michigan: Cranbrook Institute of Science, 1940), 97 pp.

18. Stuart, Laurence C. (zoology). (a) "Studies of Neo-tropical Colubrinae. VIII. A Revision

of the Genus Dryadophis Stuart, 1939," *Miscellaneous Publications of the Museum of Zoology, University of Michigan,* 49 (1941), 106 pp. (*b*) "The Amphibians and Reptiles of Alta Verapaz, Guatemala," *ibid.,* 69 (1948), 109 pp. (*c*) "A Geographic Study of the Herpetofauna of Alta Verapaz, Guatemala," *Contributions from the Laboratory of Vertebrate Biology, University of Michigan,* 45 (1950), 77 pp. (*d*) "The Herpetofauna of the Guatemalan Plateau," *ibid.,* 49 (1951), 71 pp., 7 pls.

19. Sutton, George M. (zoology). (*a*) "Juvenal Plumage and Post-Juvenal Molt of the Vesper Sparrow," *Occasional Papers, Museum of Zoology, University of Michigan,* 445 (1941), 10 pp., with colored plate of a painting by the author. (*b*) "The Plumages and Molts of the Young Eastern Whippoorwill," *ibid.,* 446 (1941), 6 pp., with colored plate of a painting by the author.

20. Trautman, Milton B. (zoology). "The Birds of Buckeye Lake, Ohio," *Miscellaneous Publications of the Museum of Zoology, University of Michigan,* 44 (1940), 466 pp.

21. van der Schalie, Henry (zoology). (*a*) Volume II of the Index to *The Nautilus* (1886–present). (In preparation). (*b*) "The Land and Fresh-Water Mollusks of Puerto Rico," *Miscellaneous Publications of the Museum of Zoology, University of Michigan,* 70 (1948), 128 pp., 4 figs., 14 pls., 64 maps.

22. Wagner, Warren H., Jr. (botany). "Types of Foliar Dichotomy in Living Ferns," *American Journal of Botany,* XXXIX (1952), pp. 578–92.

23. Wehmeyer, Lewis E. (botany). (*a*) "Perithecial Development in Pleospora Trichostoma" (accepted for publication by the *Botanical Gazette*). (*b*) "Studies in the Genus Pleospora—VI," *American Journal of Botany,* XXXIX (1952), pp. 237–43. (*c*) "The Genera Leptosphaeria, Pleospora, and Clathrospora in Mt. Rainier National Park," *Mycologia,* XLIV (1952), pp. 621–55.

(III) THE SOCIAL SCIENCES AND RELATED FIELDS

1. Aiton, Arthur S. (history). *The Muster Roll and Equipment of the Expedition of Francisco Vazquez de Coronado* (Ann Arbor: William L. Clements Library [Bulletin No. XXX], 1939), 28 pp.

2. Bond, Floyd A. (economics). "Public Regulation in Action: A Study of the Experience of a Michigan Gas Company," *University of Michigan Bureau of Government, Michigan Governmental Studies,* No. 17 (1948), ix+212 pp.

3. Davis, Charles Moler (geography). "Survey of Transfer Admission in American Colleges and Universities," *University of Michigan Administrative Studies,* I, No. 4 (1942), 53 pp.

4. Donahue, Wilma, with Clyde H. Coombs and Robert M. W. Travers (eds.) (psychology). *Guidance Conference in the Measurement of Student Achievement and Adjustment* (Ann Arbor: University of Michigan Press, 1949), 256 pp.

5. Dwyer, Paul S. (mathematics), with Charlotte S. Horner and Clarence S. Yoakum (psychology). "A Statistical Summary of Records of Students Entering the University of Michigan as Freshmen in the Decade 1927–1936," *University of Michigan Administrative Studies,* I, No. 4 (1940), v+226 pp.

6. Ford, Robert S. (Bureau of Government). "Realty Tax Delinquency in Michigan," *University of Michigan Bureau of Government, New Series Bulletin,* No. 18 (1937), vi+125 pp.
   Ford, Robert S. (ed.) (Bureau of Government). "A Manual of State Administrative Organization in Michigan," *University of Michigan Bureau of Government, Michigan Governmental Studies,* No. 4 (1940), 240 pp.
   Ford, Robert S., and Marvin A. Bacon (Bureau of Government). "Michigan Highway Finance," *University of Michigan Bureau of Government, Michigan Governmental Studies,* No. 12 (1943), 191 pp.

7. Grace, Frank (political science), "The Concept of Property in Modern Christian Thought," *Illinois Studies in the Social Sciences*, XXXIV, Nos. 1 and 2 (1953), ix+173 pp.

8. Greenman, Emerson F. (anthropology). "Old Birch Island Cemetery and the Early Historic Trade Route, Georgian Bay, Ontario," *Occasional Contributions from the Museum of Anthropology, University of Michigan*, 11 (1951), viii+69 pp.

9. Griffin, James B., with Philip Phillips and James A. Ford (anthropology). "Archaeological Survey in the Lower Mississippi Alluvial Valley 1940–47," *Papers of the Peabody Museum of American Archaeology and Ethnology, Harvard University*, 25 (1951), xii+472 pp., 113 figs.

10. Griffin, James B. (anthropology). *The Fort Ancient Aspect: Its Cultural and Chronological Position in the Mississippi Valley Archaeology* (Ann Arbor: University of Michigan Press, 1943), xv+392 pp.

11. Hall, Robert B. (geography). *Atlas of the Japanese Empire* (in progress).

12. Hawley, Amos H. (sociology). (*a*) "The Population of Michigan, 1840 to 1960—An Analysis of Growth, Distribution and Composition," *University of Michigan Bureau of Government, Michigan Governmental Studies*, No. 19 (1949), 116 pp. (*b*) "Intrastate Migration in Michigan: 1935–1940," *Ibid.*, No. 25 (1953), 196 pp.

13. Husselman, Elinor M. (archaeology). "A Boharic School Text on Papyrus," *Journal of Near Eastern Studies*, 6 (1947), pp. 129–51.

14. Kinietz, W. Vernon (anthropology). "The Indians of the Western Great Lakes, 1615–1750," *Occasional Contributions from the Museum of Anthropology, University of Michigan*, 10 (1940), xiv+427 pp.

15. Krogman, Wilton M. (anthropology). "A Study of Four Skulls from Seleucia-on-the-Tigris dating from 100 B.C. to 200 A.D.," *Human Biology*, 12 (1940), pp. 313–22.

16. Litchfield, Edward H. (political science). "Voting Behavior in a Metropolitan Area." *University of Michigan Bureau of Government, Michigan Governmental Studies*, No. 7 (1941), vii+93 pp.

17. Lobanov-Rostovsky, Andrei (history). *Russia and Europe 1825–1878* (To be released by George Wahr Publishing Company, 1954), 302 pp.

18. Maier, Norman R. F., with N. M. Glaser (psychology). "Studies of Abnormal Behavior in the Rat. II. A Comparison of Some Convulsion Producing Situations," *Comparative Psychology Monographs*, 16 (1940), 30 pp.

19. Perkins, John A. (political science). "The Role of the Governor of Michigan in the Enactment of Appropriations," *University of Michigan Bureau of Government, Michigan Governmental Studies*, No. 11 (1943), ix+197 pp.

20. Pollock, James (political science). (*a*) "Permanent Registration of Voters in Michigan—the Iniative and Referendum," *University of Michigan Bureau of Government, New Series Bulletin* No. 7 (1937), 15 pp. (*b*) "Voting Behavior: A Case Study," *University of Michigan Bureau of Government, Michigan Governmental Studies*, No. 3 (1939), 40 pp. (*c*) "The Initiative and Referendum in Michigan," *ibid.*, No. 6 (1940), 100 pp. (*d*) "Direct Government in Michigan," *University of Michigan Bureau of Government Pamphlet*, No. 8 (1940), 20 pp. (*e*) "Michigan Politics in Transition," *University of Michigan Bureau of Government, Michigan Governmental Studies*, No. 10 (1942), 74 pp. (*f*) "The Direct Primary in Michigan, 1900–1935," *Ibid.*, No. 14 (1943), 81 pp.

21. Riegel, John W. (industrial relations). *The Selection and Development of Foremen* (Ann Arbor: University of Michigan Press, 1941), 69 pp.

22. Shepard, E. Fenton, and William B. Wood. "The Financing of Public Schools in Michigan," University of Michigan Bureau of Government, Michigan Governmental Studies, No. 13 (1943), 135 pp.

23. Tharp, Claude R. (Bureau of Government). (a) "A Manual of City Government in Michigan," *University of Michigan Bureau of Government, Michigan Governmental Studies,* No. 22 (1951), 175 pp. (b) "A Manual of Village Government in Michigan," *ibid.,* No. 23 (1951), 118 pp.

(IV) LANGUAGE AND LITERATURE

1. Brown, Lloyd A. (Clements Library). (a) *Jean Domenique Cassini and His World Map of 1696* (Ann Arbor: University of Michigan Press, 1941), 79 pp. (b) *Notes on the Care and Cataloguing of Old Maps* (Windham, Connecticut: Hawthorn House, 1948), 110 pp.

2. Clements Library. *The Netherlands and America, A Clements Library Bulletin Prepared on the Hundredth Anniversary of the Establishment of the City of Holland in Michigan* (Ann Arbor: University of Michigan Press, 1947), 64 pp.

3. Denkinger, Marc (French). *Essentials of French Pronunciation; A New Approach* (Ann Arbor: George Wahr Publishing Company, 1952), 169 pp.

4. Kilgour, Raymond L. (library science). *Messrs. Roberts Brothers, Publishers* (Ann Arbor: University of Michigan Press, 1952), xv+307 pp.

5. McCartney, Eugene S. (classics). "Greek and Roman References to the Netting of Quail Migrating Across the Mediterranean Sea," *Papers of the Michigan Academy,* 25 (1940), pp. 543–52.

6. Ogden, Henry V. S., and Margaret S. Ogden (English). *English Taste in Landscape 1600–1700* (accepted for publication, University of Michigan Press).

7. Philippson, Ernst A. (German). "Der Germanische Mütter- und Matronenkult am Niederrhein," *Germanic Review,* 19 (1944), pp. 81–142.

8. Sanchez y Escribano, Federico (Spanish). *Cosas y Casos de los albores del siglo XVII en España* (New York: Hispanic Institute in the United States, 1951), 157 pp.
Sanchez y Escribano, Federico, and Dornell H. Roaten (Spanish). *Wölfflin's Principles in Spanish Drama 1500–1700* (New York: Hispanic Institute in the United States, 1952), ix+200 pp.

9. Scanio, Vincent A. (Italian). "Collezione Giordani of the Biblioteca Communale dell'Archiginnasio. A Supplementary Bibliography," *Italica,* 23 (1946), pp. 189–236.

10. Tilley, Morris P. (English). *A Dictionary of the Proverbs in England in the Sixteenth and Seventeenth Centuries* (Ann Arbor: University of Michigan Press, 1950), xiii+854 pp.

11. Waterman, Leroy (semitics). *Religion Faces the World Crisis* (Ann Arbor: George Wahr Publishing Company, 1943), x+206 pp.

12. Worrell, William H. (ed.) (classics). *Coptic Texts in the University of Michigan Collection.* "University of Michigan Studies, Humanistic Series," XLVI (Ann Arbor: University of Michigan Press; London: Humphrey Milford, Oxford University Press, 1942), xiv+375 pp.

13. Youtie, Herbert C., and Orsamus M. Pearl (eds.) (classics). *Papyri and Ostraca from Karanis.* "University of Michigan Studies, Humanistic Series," XLVII (Ann Arbor: University of Michigan Press; London: Humphrey Milford, Oxford University Press, 1944), xx+252 pp.
Youtie, Herbert C., and John G. Winter (eds.) (classics). *Papyri and Ostraca from Karanis, Second Series.* "University of Michigan Studies, Humanistic Series," L (Ann Arbor: University of Michigan Press; London: Geoffrey Cumberlege, Oxford University Press, 1951), xxii+266 pp.

(V) THE FINE ARTS

1. Cuyler, Louise E. (music). (*a*) *Heinrich Isaac's Choralis Constantinus, Book III. Transcribed from the Formschneider First Edition, Nürnberg 1555* (Ann Arbor: University of Michigan Press, 1950), x+456 pp. (*b*) *Five Masses of Heinrich Isaac* (accepted for publication, University of Michigan Press).
2. Wethey, Harold E. (fine arts). *Colonial Architecture and Sculpture in Peru* (Cambridge, Massachusetts: Harvard University Press, 1949), xvii+330 pp.

(VI) THE HEALTH SCIENCES

1. Anderson, Odin W. (public health). "Administration of Medical Care, Problems and Issues; Based on an Analysis of the Medical-Dental Care Program for the Recipients of Old-age Assistance in the State of Washington, 1941–1945," *Research Series, Bureau of Public Health Economics, University of Michigan,* No. 2 (1947), xv+179 pp.
2. Bodian, David T. (anatomy). (*a*) "Studies on the Diencephalon of the Virginia Opossum. I. The Nuclear Pattern in the Adult," *Journal of Comparative Neurology,* 71 (1939), pp. 259–312. (*b*) "Studies on the Diencephalon of the Virginia Opossum. II. The Fiber Connections in Normal and Experimental Material," *ibid.,* 72 (1940), pp. 207–84.
3. Crosby, Elizabeth C., and T. Humphrey (anatomy). "Studies in the Vertebrate Telencephalon," *Journal of Comparative Neurology,* 71 (1939), pp. 121–213.
4. Gaughran, George R. L. (anatomy). "A Comparative Study of the Osteology and Myology of the Cranial and Cervical Regions of the Shrew, Blarina Brevicauda, and the Mole, Scalopus Aquaticus." *Miscellaneous Publications of the Museum of Zoology, University of Michigan,* 80 (to be published in 1954).
5. Rinker, George Clark (anatomy). "The Comparative Myology of the Mammalian Genera Sigmodon, Oryzomys, Neotoma, and Peromyscus (Cricetinae)," *Miscellaneous Publications of the Museum of Zoology, University of Michigan,* 83 (to be published in 1954).
6. Scharenberg, Konstantin (psychiatry). "Atrophy of the Cerebellum Following Pressure," *Journal of Neuropathology and Experimental Neurology,* XII (1953), pp. 11–23.
7. Woodburne, Russell T. (anatomy). "Certain Phylogenetic Anatomical Relations of Localizing Significance for the Mammalian Central Nervous System," *Journal of Comparative Neurology,* 71 (1939), pp. 215–57.

Notes

[1] Keith T. Sward, *The Legend of Henry Ford* (Chicago, 1948), p. 18.

[2] James Martin Miller, *The Amazing Story of Henry Ford* (Chicago, 1922), p. 73.

[3] Henry Ford, *My Life and Work* (New York, 1922), pp. 51–52.

[4] The Trustees gave the University's Egyptian project $25,000 in May, 1934, and $25,000 in June, 1935. The second gift was transferred, with the Trustees' consent, to further the University's diggings at Seleucia in Asia Minor.

[5] Of about $16,611,000 in the Horace H. Rackham estate, $11,187,000 went for bequests, taxes, and legal fees, but in the six-and-a-half years of the Trustees' administration, which began in the depression of the 1930's, the property increased in value by about $7,702,000. Moreover, the United States government refunded to the Rackham estate $713,000, having finally lost a suit for taxes on the 1919 sale of Ford stock. The case was won by Clarence E. Wilcox, who had joined Rackham and Anderson in 1905. He was one of the Trustees of Mr. Rackham's estate and one of the first three members of the Board of Governors of the Horace H. Rackham School of Graduate Studies, of which he is still a member.

[6] Trustees named in Mr. Rackham's will were: his wife, Mary A. Rackham; his brother-in-law, Bryson D. Horton; his law partners, Clarence E. Wilcox and Arthur J. Lacy; and his secretary, Miss Mabel Cameron. The last two resigned almost immediately and were replaced by Mrs. Myra H. Bussey, a sister of Mrs. Rackham and Mr. Horton, and Mr. Frederick G. Rolland, Mr. Rackham's lifelong friend.

[7] See Appendix I, page 77.

[8] Officially so named and established "under the immediate direction of the Executive Board of the Graduate School" by the Regents, April 30, 1937.

[9] Later enlarged to: the Dean, the Director, and six members of the University Senate. This grew out of an Advisory Committee, initiated March 30, 1939.

[10] This project produced *Integrating the Camp, the Community and Social Work*, by Lowell Juilliard Carr, Mildred Aileen Valentine, and Marshall H. Levy (New York: Association Press, 1939), 220 pp.

[11] In 1938 the $1,000 received from the Michigan Child Guidance Institute was applied toward the remodeling of the house at 1027 East Huron Street.

[12] University of Michigan Press (1949), 256 pp.

[13] On October 1, 1947, Dr. Donahue, as Director of the Psychological Clinic, received a grant of $5,200 from the Jennie Grogan Mendelson Memorial Fund, Detroit, to make a psychological study of the effectiveness of an electronic reader for the blind. In 1949 and 1950 the Veterans Administration supported this project with a $42,000 contract.

[14] "Report on the Parking Survey of the Flint Downtown Business District," *University of Michigan, Social Science Research Project* (November, 1950), pp. 1–32.

[15] These early plans led to a laboratory project on aging and heredity, supported from 1940 until 1949 with some $80,000 from the Horace H. Rackham Fund and headed by Professor Lee R. Dice. The project began with a study of heredity, and research on aging was postponed.

[16] One of the first three was edited by Clark Tibbitts; the other two, by Clark Tibbitts and Wilma Donahue; the fourth, by Wilma Donahue, James Rae, Jr., and Roger Berry. All four books were published by the University of Michigan Press.

[17] The Unit receives outside funds from the United States Public Health Service and the Michigan Arthritis and Rheumatism Foundation; and from the Eli Lilly Company (a pharmaceutical firm) for research in gout.

[18] Another member of the Horton family, Mrs. Mabel F. Patterson, was not a Rackham Trustee.

[19] Dedication issue of *The Foundation*, The Engineering Society of Detroit, Vol. VI, No. 5 (January, 1942), p. 4.

[20] *Ibid.*, p. 5.

[21] In March and May, 1935, the McGregor Foundation of Washington, D.C., and the Horace H. Rackham and Mary A. Rackham Fund each contributed $10,000 to an Institute of the Health and Social Sciences, which was to conduct regular University Extension Courses in Detroit. The McGregor Foundation continued major yearly support, which was supplemented by the United States Public Health Service, until the end of fiscal year 1943–44. The Trustees of the Rackham estate, who had collaborated in founding the Institute, by specific provision, housed it (redesignated the Institute of Public and Social Administration, on May 15, 1936) in the new Horace H. Rackham Educational Memorial, and the Board of Governors of the Graduate School supported it with $8,000 for the year 1936–37. Later, the Rackham-supported Bureau of Reference and Research in Government (see page 37) became a part of the (again redesignated) Institute of Public Administration.

[22] Detroit Engineering Society, $547,189.11; the University of Michigan, $750,057.55.

[23] Minutes of the Board of Governors, Vol. II, p. 110.

[24] In 1929, he had received a grant of $22,000 a year for three years from the Children's Fund of Michigan for that purpose.

[25] His most recent publication, as Emeritus Dean of the School of Dentistry, is *The Story of Dental Caries* (Ann Arbor: Overbeck Co., 1953), 94 pp.

[26] *Property Tax Limitation Laws,* Public Administration Series, No. 36, 1934, pp. 62–66.

[27] In the following description, space is not intended as a measure of the value of the research. The sums listed for individual grants are, in most cases, the amounts spent, rather than the amounts of the grants.

[28] With James T. Wilson, *Papers of the Michigan Academy of Sciences, Arts, and Letters,* Vol. 29 (1944), pp. 345–54.

[29] Kenneth K. Landes, George M. Ehlers, and George M. Stanley, *Geology of the Mackinac Straits Region and Sub-surface Geology of the Northern Part of the Southern Peninsula,* Publication 44, Geological Series 37, State of Michigan Department of Conservation (Lansing, 1945), 204 pp.

[30] From Professor Stanley's request for Rackham funds.

[31] "Partial Pyrolysis of Wood" (with Robert W. Merritt), *Industrial and Engineering Chemistry,* Vol. 35 (1943), p. 297.

[32] Donald L. Katz, G. W. Preskshot, N. G. Delisle, and C. E. Cottrell, "Asphaltic Substances in Crude Oils," *Transactions of the American Institute of Mechanical Engineers,* Vol. 151 (1942), pp. 188–205.

[33] With M. J. Raza (Ann Arbor: Edwards Brothers, Inc., 1946), 306 pp.

[34] *The President's Report for 1927–1928* (University of Michigan), p. 302.

[35] Leo Goldberg, editor, *The Structure of the Galaxy* (University of Michigan Press, 1951), 84 pp., illus.

[36] Karl G. Henize and Dean B. McLaughlin, "The Spectrum of Nova Pictoris, 1925," *Publications of the Astronomical Society of the Pacific,* Vol. 62, No. 368 (October, 1950).

[37] *Regents Proceedings,* 1929–1932, p. 859.

[38] May 31, 1935: $20,000; February 28, 1936: $5,000.

[39] *President's Report for 1934–1935* (University of Michigan), p. 213.

[40] *Ibid.*

[41] University of Michigan Press.

[42] "Studies on the Structure of Thin Metallic Films by Means of the Electron Microscope" (with Robert G. Picard), *Journal of Applied Physics,* Vol. 14 (1943), pp. 291–305, 25 figs., 4 tab.

[43] "Momentum Distribution of Charged Cosmic-Ray Particles at Sea Level" (with B. Hamermest and G. Safonov), *The Physical Review,* Vol. 80 (1950), pp. 1069–75, 8 figs.

[44] "Shower Production by Penetrating Particles at 14,000 Feet" (with H. S. Bridge), *The Physical Review,* Vol. 74 (1948), pp. 57–88, 4 figs.

"A Study of Cosmic-Ray Bursts" (with H. S. Bridge, B. Rossi, and R. W. Williams), *ibid.,* pp. 1083–1102, 24 figs.

"The Vertical Intensity at 10,000 Feet of Ionizing Particles That Produce Penetrating Showers" (with C. A. Randall and O. L. Tiffany), *ibid.,* Vol. 75 (1949), pp. 694–95.

[45] With O. L. Tiffany, *The Physical Review,* Vol. 77 (1950), p. 849.

[46] With C. A. Randall and N. Sherman, *The Physical Review,* Vol. 79 (1950), p. 905.

[47] With C. A. Randall, *The Physical Review,* Vol. 81 (1951), 144–45.

[48] University of Michigan Press (1943), xx+785 pp., 634 figs.

[49] University of Michigan Press (1950), xv+227 pp., frontis., 79 pls. The quotation comes from the endorsement by Professor William C. Steere (chairman of the Department of Botany) of Professor Taylor's request.

[50] See page 20 and footnote 15.

[51] See page 24.

[52] *Bulletin of the Cranbrook Institute of Science,* XXVI (1947), xi+186 pp., 26 col. pls., 289 figs.

[53] See page 2.

[54] This figure includes the $12,000 granted in this category to Mr. Harold D. Smith for the Bureau of Reference and Research in Government (1936–37). See page 37.

[55] This sum was augmented by extensive assistance from the National Youth Administration. For other work by Professor Pollock, see page 67.

[56] Lowell Juilliard Carr and James Edson Stenner, *Willow Run; a Study of Industrialization and Cultural Inadequacy* (New York: Harper's Social Science Series, 1952), 406 pp.

[57] See Table II, page 38.

[58] See page 42.

[59] See page 64.

[60] James K. Pollock and Homer Thomas, with the assistance and collaboration of Willett F. Ramsdell, William C. Trow, and Manfred C. Vernon, *Germany in Power and Eclipse* (New York, Toronto and London: D. Van Nostrand Company, Inc., 1952), 661 pp.

[61] University of Michigan Press (1950), x+456 pp.

[62] *Campanology, Europe 1945–47* (University of Michigan Press, 1948), vii+161 pp.

[63] See page 2.

[64] See page 37.

[65] See page 58.

[66] See page 20.

[67] See Table II, page 38 and page 73.

[68] See page 77.

[69] See page 72.

Printed and bound by CPI Group (UK) Ltd, Croydon, CR0 4YY

13/04/2025

14656541-0002